Ellen Mackubin

The King of the Town

Ellen Mackubin

The King of the Town

ISBN/EAN: 9783743312357

Manufactured in Europe, USA, Canada, Australia, Japa

Cover: Foto ©ninafisch / pixelio.de

Manufactured and distributed by brebook publishing software (www.brebook.com)

Ellen Mackubin

The King of the Town

THE KING OF THE TOWN

BY

ELLEN MACKUBIN

BOSTON AND NEW YORK
HOUGHTON, MIFFLIN AND COMPANY
The Riverside Press, Cambridge
M DCCC XCVIII

Copyright, 1898,
BY ELLEN MACKUBIN.

All rights reserved.

THIS STORY IS DEDICATED

TO

MY MOTHER.

E. M.

THE KING OF THE TOWN

I

Fort Ludlow is one of the oldest posts in Montana. It is also one of the smallest. Established for the maintenance of order on an Indian reservation a few miles distant, it has survived the departure of the nation's wards, and the opening of their lands to settlers.

Rumors of rich mining probabilities attracted these invaders in hordes, and Fort Ludlow promptly discovered that they were likely to require more constant watchfulness than its former charges. The post commanders had been wont to find pleasure in much grumbling concerning the anxiety resulting from the wiles of agents and the restlessness of redskins. But, during the year which had elapsed since the little mushroom town sprang into existence, fervent had been their regrets for the change of responsibility. Puritans and saints the lamented savages were asserted to appear when compared with the outcasts of civilization who had been substituted for those gentle neighbors by the starting of two silver mines, and the building of a branch railroad which connected with the Northern Pacific.

Heedless of the anxiety it inspired, and engrossed by its own struggle for life, Silverton thus far had manifested scant interest in its guardian fort beyond a tendency among certain professional gamblers and keepers of drinking saloons to ensnare unwary troopers to the loss of pay and the overstaying of furloughs. Nor, in spite of wild fightings and brawlings, had it shown any tendency to that direct appeal to military protection without which a paternal government does not permit soldiers to prevent civilians from cutting each other's throats when they are so inclined.

Time passed smoothly and rather sluggishly at Ludlow, where the small society was composed chiefly of married people, and where special effort for gayety was forbidden by the recent sorrow which had brought their only young lady to make her home with her brother, Captain Lorimer, and his wife.

In such a community events were rare boons, and the installation of a new commanding officer was of equal social and military importance.

Major Cornish had been promoted from another regiment. His future associates knew of him merely his age, that he was unmarried, and that he had achieved distinction during several campaigns in Arizona. Much, therefore, was the curiosity, and many the predictions, which anticipated his coming.

Within twenty-four hours of his arrival, the officers of the garrison had been formally presented to him by Captain Lorimer, acting commandant since the departure of

Major Wharton. Every lady had made his acquaintance at "band-play"—and the characteristics of his outward man and manner were matters of defined if diverse public opinion.

Very soldierly, rather silent, and looking fully his thirty-six years, was the sum of Edith Lorimer's first impressions. That his steadfast blue eyes would, on further observation, prove to be more grave than stern, was a corollary, presumably correct, and defended against the opinion of the surgeon's wife, that they were eyes to which she could never talk freely,—an assertion which Mrs. Blount's friends would have found incredible, for reasons quite apart from the quality of Major Cornish's regard.

The incessant chatter of that voluble lady, and the equally incessant jolting of the ambulance, which was the substitute for a closed carriage at Ludlow, speedily reduced Edith's share in the conversation to monosyllables. Their drive to Silverton had been undertaken for shopping purposes, valued principally by the feminine portion of the garrison as being a privilege only granted to them by their husbands and brothers since certain recent reforms in the street decorum of the settlement. Usually, the "general stores," among which that shopping had to be done, constituted a lottery where the prizes were few. But on this afternoon their errands proved unwontedly successful, and packages were heaped upon the benches of the ambulance as they passed through the gates of the post on their return.

Edith glanced wistfully at the windows of her brother's quarters, when the soldier-driver pulled up the four mules before the door. Neither she nor Mrs. Blount had outgrown their natural fear of those unsubjugated animals, and neither would permit the driver to leave them. No sign of help, however, was to be perceived from behind the muslin custains, of whose dainty conventionality Edith's sister-in-law was justly proud.

She poised herself anxiously upon the

single lofty step of the ambulance, and gathering her skirts free of the enormous wheels, she prepared to take the necessary leap.

"Allow me to assist you, Miss Lorimer," a pleasant, unfamiliar voice exclaimed. "Will you put your hands on my shoulders? So!"

And she swiftly descended to earth in the stalwart arms of Major Cornish.

"This does n't seem an equipage exactly adapted for ladies," he said, lifting his cap to Mrs. Blount.

"Don't say a word against it, please," she implored. "If you find fault it will be taken from us, and we shall never get over to Silverton!"

"Is the town so attractive? From what I saw as I rode through it last night, I should not have thought that you could be trusted there without escort."

"Edith, dear! He is going to be a tyrant! He means to take away our few hard-won privileges," Mrs. Blount cried pathetically.

"Rather a supplicant than a tyrant! I spoke of an escort, hoping that I might sometimes belong to its number."

"Except for the pleasure of it, nobody needs an escort in Silverton since the reign of Dare has begun," Edith said, returning from the house followed by the "striker," who collected her share of the parcels.

"Who is Dare?" Cornish asked.

"The 'king of the town,'" Mrs. Blount cried gayly. "Miss Lorimer will be delighted to tell you about him. She is one of his champions. Good-by!"

Thereupon the ambulance driver shook the reins, and, after a playful pretense of preferring the sidewalk to the roadway, which forced Edith to the doorstep, the mules trotted briskly along the parade.

"'The king of the town'? That description is what novelists call suggestive," Cornish said with a smile which Edith liked, in spite of its gleam of irony. "I shall hope to hear more of 'his majesty' this evening, as Mrs. Lorimer has asked me to dine."

"I will introduce the subject, but my brother's eloquence shall continue it," she said lightly. "He declares that this Dare is the very ally a commandant at Ludlow requires to help him in keeping peace among those miners."

"Then it behooves me to learn what terms this ally will condescend to make," he replied.

She turned away a little abruptly. Irony in a smile, she decided, like vinegar in a salad, was an element dangerous to the charm of the whole, unless used with a discretion which was unfortunately rare!

Nevertheless she dressed for dinner, conscious of keener anticipation of interest than for many months. She had not dwelt thus long among her present surroundings without discovering that the prejudices of a commanding officer influence those of his subordinates in lines not considered by army regulations; and she believed that Major Cornish's support would be necessary to the success of a plan on which she assured herself that her happiness at Ludlow depended.

Edith Lorimer had come to this new home in a mood which was more impressed by its narrowness than by the novelty which presents garrison life picturesquely to most girl visitors. During several previous years she had been the close and confidential companion of her father, a man whose successful literary career had been in touch with all that was finest of the world's progress. After such a past, the present of a three-company post sauntering through the monotony of these peaceful days, with a round of limited duties, limited pleasures, and yet more limited interests, seemed a blank desolation. Her heart, moreover, was yet lonelier than her mind. A father's affection had hitherto held her obviously first, while now, though Tom and Dorothy were very kind, they sufficed for each other's happiness. They and their wonderful baby! Her heart felt empty, her hands idle, and the wistful desire had grown that she might fill this emptiness and employ this idleness with work that should help such needs as neighbored the state of life into which she had been newly led. Such work as she had seen girls of her own class accomplish in the worst districts of New York, she thought herself capable of achieving among the wretched women and children whom she occasionally saw in her rapid flittings through Silverton. But she was aware that Tom, who possessed the usual masculine aversion for any project likely to thrust publicity on a wife or a sister, would oppose this scheme, unless she secured for it so influential a favor as that of his commanding officer.

Edith's bright eyes, fair hair, and fresh complexion were of the type which sober colors best become. Nothing could have suited her more daintily than the black gauze through which her neck and arms shone whitely. Nor was she, despite recent sorrow and serious purpose, without sustaining content in that knowledge, as she walked downstairs to the drawing-room.

This drawing-room reflected greater credit upon its mistress than would any of the gorgeous apartments designed and executed by some fashionable firm of decorators belonging to far-distant civilization. The cretonne hangings were Dorothy's own handiwork. The many-cushioned divan had been a packing-case, covered and padded by her skillful fingers. Tablecloths, mantel draperies, — even the frames of the etchings and engravings which almost hid the whitewashed walls, — were Dorothy's creations. She still regretted the decorators, though she was proud of her success; but her husband's pride was marred by no regret whatever. Edith found him detailing to Cornish the origin of many a quaint contrivance, and relating the adventures through which boxes of china and his wife's beloved piano had survived the varied dangers of prairie freight transportation.

She liked the manner of Cornish's listening to a subject which progressed to the dinner-table and threatened to exclude any other. His blue eyes could be very kindly, and his smile, despoiled of irony, was worth some trouble to provoke. But she grew impatient, after a while, of Tom's narratives, which aroused mutinous memories of days when he had displayed a too masterful interest in the equipment of her doll's house. The topic she desired was, however, finally brought forward by Dorothy, who declared that no future housekeeper setting up an establishment at Ludlow would realize how bare the land had been upon her arrival.

"Why, Tom would not allow me to shop in Silverton except under escort of himself and a couple of revolvers that frightened away the remembrance of my errands!" she said, laughing; "even if it had been possible to find anything I wanted before Mr. Dare opened his 'general store.'"

"Dolly, you have proposed my toast," Edith exclaimed gayly, meeting the glance with which Cornish reminded her of her promise. "Tom, I told Major Cornish that you would explain to him what Mr. Dare is doing in Silverton."

"What Dare is doing?" Lorimer repeated, while his cheery countenance became serious. "That subject will stretch beyond table-talk. He has made a remarkable beginning, and the end is not yet in sight."

"I have heard him mentioned by three people to-day," Cornish said, "each one of whom has suggested a different character. What is he? Shop-keeper, adventurer, missionary? — or a combination of all three, which may produce that first emanation from chaos in Western towns — 'a leading citizen'?"

"You have hit him off very nearly, except that in Dare's case the missionary preponderates to an extent which is likely to develop the leading citizen into a martyr instead of a member of Congress, which is the usual ultimate evolution when we become sufficiently civilized to be annexed."

"A martyr? Nowadays?" Cornish exclaimed lightly.

"Why not?"

"Because martyrdom requires simpler

faith and more strenuous conviction than exists in these days of complexity and uncertainty."

"We are centuries behind our generation out here!" Tom laughed. "There is nothing simpler or more convinced in the history of the 'dark ages' than public opinion and private practice in Silverton — and this Dare," he continued, growing earnest again, "this Dare hurls himself against those opinions and those practices as fearlessly as — who was that Florentine chap, Edith?"

"Savonarola?"

"Savonarola, yes! So it seems to me not improbable that his fate will be the same — with the substitution of a 'six-shooter' for a stake and flames."

"Yet Miss Lorimer tells me that you think this picturesquely tragic individual would make a useful ally for us in bringing law and order to the town?"

"Exactly. His enthusiasm needs only to be moderated by discretion to achieve an object which is in part the same as ours."

"Do you suggest that the chief characteristic of the army is discretion?" Dorothy exclaimed as indignantly as though Tom had slandered her beloved soldiers.

"We must be strategists when it is necessary," Cornish interposed with a smile. "Does this Dare preach?"

"Come and hear him," Edith said eagerly. "He preaches twice each week outside his store, and my brother has promised to take me there again to-morrow."

"Thank you, I shall be delighted. But street preaching, according to general opinion, is more likely to produce disorder than the reverse."

Lorimer leaned forward impressively.

"I assure you, Major, that, turbulent and dissolute as the settlement seems to you, it is a land of Beulah compared to the moral piggery this fellow found it when he arrived six months ago. The place is more a mining camp than a town even yet, for there is no civil authority. But Dare is rapidly assuming the position of 'regulator.'"

"Dangerous, I should say."

"Not while the uprightness of his aims is so obvious."

"How does he manifest it?"

"By half a dozen methods. He has established behind his store what might be called a club, if it were not a ' free for all ' luxury. Men can get drink there in moderation, with billiards, newspapers, and magazines. But neither drunkenness nor gambling is permitted."

"How are they forbidden?"

"Dare and his barkeeper wear revolvers, which nobody doubts that they would use if needful."

"Rather violent for a missionary."

"Violent ills require violent remedies," Tom quoted. "Silverton leading strings must be made of stout stuff."

"He wants to open a small hospital for the victims of accidents and shooting frays," Edith said.

"Is he wealthy?"

"I fancy most of his money is in the

store, which my wife has told you is also a boon to the town."

"He is a many-sided phenomenon!"

"Perhaps you will find his first appearance here theatrical!" Edith exclaimed indignantly. "He volunteered to lead a rescue party, after an explosion at the 'Spread Eagle' mine."

"Did I not say that he is many-sided?" Cornish asked undismayed. "You add heroism to the various aspects we have already considered."

"There is another," Dorothy, who was slightly bored, declared, smiling as she rose. "He is well bred, well educated, and the handsomest man I have ever seen!"

Cornish opened the door for the exit of the ladies, and Edith, meeting his serene glance, was vexedly aware that she blushed.

Probably he would classify her in his thoughts as a schoolgirlish young person inclined to vary the dullness of Ludlow by an ardent discipleship of this picturesque adventurer.

Such a classification, though mortifying, was endurable for a few hours, and to-morrow he would do justice to her and to the cause she had adopted. No prejudice which was sincere and intelligent would withstand the earnestness of one of Dare's rough addresses, and, despite her vexation, she did not doubt that both sincerity and intelligence underlay their new commanding officer's determined aloofness from the local enthusiasm. He meant to judge for himself, but she thought he would judge fairly, and she anticipated some triumph in his conversion.

Whatever was Major Cornish's impression of her ill-timed blush, or whether he retained any impression of it, she had no chance of guessing that evening. He entered the drawing-room merely for an apologetic "good-night" after Dorothy had fallen asleep in an armchair, and Tom reported that they had found so many regimental matters to discuss that the lateness of the hour had been forgotten.

Major Cornish was middle-aged, Edith decided as she went upstairs,— a fault more incurable than boyishness, she supplemented with a remorseful smile for certain newly-fledged lieutenants toward whom she felt the tolerance natural to a clever girl of three and twenty, conscious of wider experience than her masculine cotemporaries. Yet middle age should be the epoch of common-sense and practical activity. Both these qualities would respond to a clear perception of Dare's work, and she must continue to seek from Major Cornish that approval for her own scheme which she knew would influence Tom's consent to it.

Dare's preaching had been announced for eight o'clock on the following evening, and a blithe little riding party set out immediately after dinner, composed of Tom and Edith Lorimer, Mrs. Blount, Cornish, and young Gwynne.

"It should give you painful foreboding of Ludlow dullness, Major Cornish, that we rush to a sermon as though it were an exhilarating gayety!" Mrs. Blount cried as they passed through the post gateway.

"Why not confess, as I do, that the sermon forms a small addition to the charm of a moonlight ride in such pleasant company?"

"It is the main object with some of us, I assure you. For instance, Miss Lorimer thinks the occasion too serious for the frivolity of a brisk gallop."

"Try me!" Edith exclaimed, smiling, and, touching her horse with her whip, she darted away across the billowy uplands, followed by the others.

June possessed the world, and in the western horizon lingered an afterglow, among whose ruddy glories dawned the evening star. Over the early summer freshness of the grass the happy horses bounded, and a thousand perfumy odors wrapped the senses of the riders as they swept on through the vast stillness.

"Suppose we skip the sermon and ride further?" young Gwynne entreated, when the scattered lights of the settlement twinkled before them. "Nobody will believe that the world is a bad place on such a glorious night as this! — and that is what preachers always hammer into us."

Tom Lorimer, however, had a purpose, and he announced it.

"This party means business," he declared. "The sooner the commandant at Ludlow makes acquaintance with the king of the town the better for the subjects of both potentates! Therefore to the sermon we go!"

And, after some laughing protests, his companions acquiesced.

Silverton, as has been said, was yet a mining camp rather than a town, though its citizens would have been dangerously affronted by the suggestion.

It consisted of a long wide street, on either side of which straggled edifices that bore evidence in varying degree to flimsiness of material and hastiness of construction, the most primitive being of canvas stretched dingily over timbers, while the more substantial frame houses were painted in gaudy colors which expressed the vivid tastes of their owners. The sheds and offices of the mines which formed the *raison d'être* of the settlement loomed darkly at each extremity of the street, and between were the dwellings of the miners, a somewhat startling number of drinking saloons, a couple of stores, and at the further end the low buildings and freight cars of the railway station.

On the doorsteps of their lodgings lounged rough-looking men and slatternly women, while through some lighted windows came the sound of dance music and shouts of coarse laughter. But there were fewer loafers, and the place was quieter than when Cornish had passed through it two nights since.

"Most of the population has gathered outside Dare's store," Edith explained, when he remarked the change to her. "There is his house — the long white one.

Beyond it, toward the foothills, he usually preaches, and there we shall find the people."

An instant later they turned a corner which had obstructed their view of a large, and, considering its elements, a singularly tranquil mass of humanity. Miners and railroad laborers made up the main body of the assemblage, with a few women, perhaps a dozen troopers from Ludlow, and a fringe of cow-boy riders from the neighboring ranches.

Near one of these latter groups Tom Lorimer halted his party, and a share of the general silence fell upon them.

Occasionally a horse shook his bridle impatiently, or there was a laugh from some irrepressible joker, but the silence remained curiously unbroken, — almost as unbroken as that of a well-bred congregation in a stately church, though this crowd was composed of as ill-disciplined a lot as the Northwest could collect, and had already waited half an hour for the preacher.

A door closed sharply.

There was a simultaneous surge a step or two nearer the side entrance of the house, where a tall man had mounted a packing case.

He was tall, and this makeshift pulpit lifted him above his audience, yet the rising moon, which touched the upturned faces most remote from him, left his own invisible. He was dressed in the flannel shirt, leather breeches, and high boots worn by most of his fellow citizens, and during a moment he stood motionless.

"He is dead," he said presently. The low slow tone would have carried his words clearly further than his hearers extended, and its solemnity gave them their full import. "One of you told me yesterday that the world about you is too near and too busy to permit you to spare time for thought of the world hereafter, which seems far away! This man found the distance between these worlds barely an hour long, — and within that hour he was forced to make his preparations, as well as to do his journeying. Scant time we should find a single hour to pack our valuables and settle our responsibilities for an absence of a month or a year; this absence is for eternity. But he learned that his responsibilities had been assumed by One who paid a price for them eighteen centuries ago — And all the treasure he needed to take with him, was the belief of his repentant soul that to a dying sinner the Lord Jesus Christ said, 'This night shalt thou be with me in Paradise.'"

He paused.

Nobody stirred. Only the moon creeping upward revealed the faces nearest the pulpit, above which the preacher rose dimly, a shadow among shadows.

He began to speak more rapidly, and with increasing fervor, of the probability that many of those who listened to him must depart from the wild lives they led with as brief a warning as their comrade had received, — or with none.

"Repent!" he cried. "Repent while

your God yet waits for your repentance. The day is at hand when He shall refuse to hear, clamor you never so loudly. Then shall remain before you this journey, which is the single certainty in the future which we reckon so confidently, and you shall go forth without light, without chart, without compass, into that unfathomable darkness, that everlasting desolation which awaits those undying souls who have scorned the patience of their God."

He paused again.

The moon had found him at last, and illumined his erect figure, his wide-flung arms, his glorified countenance.

Edith suddenly remembered her hope for the conversion of Cornish, and glanced at him.

Rigid as though he beheld a vision, he stared at the preacher. But no heaven-born emotion had hardened every line of his profile until its stern gray pallor seemed cut in stone.

As Dare's clear voice rang out once more,

those rigid features flushed and quivered, while a hand fumbled at the belt where the officers of Ludlow carried a revolver when they left the post after dark.

With an instinct swifter than thought, Edith leaned forward and touched that seeking hand.

There was no recognition in the first sombre flash of the eyes which turned to her, and in which she saw depths of the strange soul of man which women of her class and generation seldom behold, — depths where beneath civilization and Christianity and nineteenth century philosophy lurk the primeval passions. An instant, the space of a dozen mad heart-beats, then Cornish started wildly. The hand she had stayed dropped to his side, and he averted his eyes.

"He — he should have had — his chance," he muttered.

With which he pulled his horse around, and, unheeding a surprised question from Lorimer, he rode off down the street, whose empty stillness stretched away whitely in the moonlight.

"What ails him? What did he say to you?" Tom asked.

But Edith found it impossible to repeat Cornish's words, or to disclose that barely restrained impulse of violence.

"He was displeased," she answered with a sense of inadequacy which gave her an hysteric desire of laughter. "Hush, Tom, these people will do worse than hiss us, if our talking disturbs them."

A warning of whose truth her brother was so aware that he obeyed it, and presently fell again under the influence of the preacher's dramatic earnestness. As the sermon progressed, however, it included practical as well as spiritual needs, and Dare gave details of his various enterprises for the public weal, and the sums required for their prosecution, with the experienced lucidity of the average missionary. One element of success in the Northwest he proved that he thoroughly understood. His work was effectively done, and it was done quickly! Twenty minutes after he mounted the packing-case he stepped down again, and was immediately surrounded by those among his audience who desired to speak with him, or to testify substantially their appreciation of his demands. Tom, declaring that he would not detain his party an instant, joined this group, while Mrs. Blount and Gwynne, released from the necessity of silence, chattered with more than their wonted cheeriness. They assured Edith that her seriousness betokened an awakening consciousness of extraordinary cause for repentance; accusations she strove to refute with a lightness which should hide from them that she had heard little of the sermon's close.

To the delight of Mrs. Blount, Tom returned, accompanied by Dare himself. Edith had met him on a couple of similar occasions, but she looked at him with new keenness while he was presented to the others.

Seen thus near, he was older and less impressive than when distance and his own mood had idealized him. Yet, worn and thin, with deep shadows under brilliant eyes, he was a handsome man, and his manner showed that his past, of which nobody in Silverton knew anything, must have had associations of refinement.

"Mr. Dare wishes to preach to the troops at Ludlow," Tom said. "I have told him that he would be very welcome."

"If there should be an objection to my preaching within the post," Dare suggested, "I can come to any point near by where it would be convenient to assemble the soldiers, and, of course, your commandant shall fix the hour for me."

"Poor, dear fellows, they ought to be grateful to you!" Mrs. Blount exclaimed. "It is awfully good of you."

"It will give me great happiness," he replied gravely.

"I'll speak to the Major to-morrow, and send an orderly with a line to you immediately," Tom said.

"If you could induce your chief," Dare began with eagerness. "He is a stranger, I believe? Major —— ?"

"Major Cornish," Tom interjected. Then, as Dare did not conclude his sentence, he added: "You were saying that if we could induce Major Cornish "—

"If you could induce — if you could induce "— Dare repeated vacantly, while blank bewilderment stared out of his dark eyes. He pressed his hand over them with an unsteady laugh. "I — I have forgotten what I meant to say."

They echoed his laugh in some embarrassment.

"You are overtired," Edith said gently. "You work too hard."

"I suppose I am tired, though I did n't realize it," Dare answered with his accustomed vigor. "I think, Captain Lorimer, if you will allow me, that I should prefer to see Major Cornish myself to-morrow about this business."

Tom assented, and, with a rather hurried "Good-night," Dare joined another group.

Tom mounted again, and they rode along

the street where the dispersing crowd gave token of reviving and riotous hilarity. None of the Ludlow party spoke until they had turned from the town to the open country.

"That was the first sign of a breakdown, I'm afraid," Tom said regretfully. "He tries to do too much."

"Yes," Mrs. Blount agreed. "My husband says that all the ills which result from our modern mania for overwork begin with these startling lapses of memory."

"There may have been special reason," Edith hesitated.

"What reason?" Mrs. Blount interrupted gayly. "It was at the mention of Major Cornish's name that he forgot what he was saying. Do you insinuate that he knows some ghastly secret concerning our Major?"

"Nonsense!" Edith replied hastily. "You remember he had been with the poor man who died, just before the sermon, and probably there was a scene which tried his nerves."

"By the way, why did Cornish leave us so abruptly?" Tom asked.

"I daresay Major Cornish when bored is more defiant than Mr. Gwynne, who didn't dare do worse than yawn prodigiously!" Edith exclaimed, fencing as well as she was able.

"If I had jumped out as the Major did, you would all have been calling me hard names before this!" Gwynne cried aggrievedly.

"We should have said that you were rude, dear boy, — which would have been justice," Mrs. Blount asserted. "But as the deserter is our commanding officer instead of a second lieutenant, we shall say that he was permissibly unceremonious, — which is military discipline!"

While this tilt of words and laughter continued, Edith rode on silently.

She had "known sorrow, and been acquainted with grief." Yet until to-night she had never met tragedy face to face. Indeed, in that skepticism regarding experiences that have not touched it which is characteristic of youth, she had doubted whether tragedy was within the potentiality of her surroundings and generation. But to-night its presence had confronted her in two blue eyes she had classed as exponents of constitutional and cultivated self-control. And Dare, whose daily life encountered danger and perplexity undauntedly, had faltered visibly at the mention of Major Cornish's name.

She lay awake, while the moon lingered on her window, wondering if Cornish would attempt explanation of his strange emotion, and what that explanation might be. Yet her thought as she fell asleep was satisfaction that the preacher of such strong words, the doer of such brave deeds as Dare, had shrunk only for one startled instant from whatever ordeal the meeting with Cornish threatened. And it was her instinctive certainty of his resolved restraint which had decided her not to secure Tom's intervention to prevent the meeting, — a decision which she had achieved after a sharp struggle between her fear of the possibly violent result of such an interview, and her sense of dishonor in revealing any knowledge or half knowledge which had come to her by chance.

II

THE most competent servant that constant instruction and patience could evolve from an Irish trooper was unworthy to be trusted with the care of Dorothy Lorimer's beloved bricabrac. In the division of lighter household labor between the sisters, this dainty task had been assigned to Edith, because the hour during which the drawing-room could be more conveniently disordered was that succeeding breakfast, when the superior necessity of Baby's bath engrossed his mother. The command had been impressed upon the "striker" that no visitors were to be admitted while Edith was thus occupied. But the well-meaning soldier possessed a mind which resembled a sieve, inasmuch that anything impressed upon it passed immediately through.

Therefore, on the day following the preaching, Edith, adorned with apron and gloves, and wielding a silk duster, turned, in certainty of unwelcome intrusion, as the door was flung open.

Cornish hesitated on the threshold with a smile whose wistfulness moved her to sudden sympathy, it was so unlike the half kindly, half ironical serenity which had slightly vexed her in such smiles as she had seen him wear hitherto.

"This is a very proud man who knows that he has betrayed what he desires to conceal — and it humiliates him," she thought swiftly.

"I had no warning that any domestic rite was in progress," he said. "You will be exceedingly kind if you can allow me to speak to you for a moment."

"By all means," she exclaimed, drawing off her gloves to give him her hand, "if you don't mind swallowing a great deal of dust! Sit there, please," she added, lifting a cover which had been stretched over a masterpiece of Dorothy's upholstery.

But Cornish did not obey. He folded

his arms on the tall back of the chair, and looked down at her, as she sat opposite him.

"Thank you for your silence concerning the exhibition I made of myself last night," he said.

"Did you imagine that I should speak of it?" she asked rather indignantly.

"I was sure that I might trust your goodness; yet few would have refrained from making public my possibilities as a melodramatic ass."

He paused, but Edith made no reply.

"You must have expected some explanation?" he said.

"I hoped that you would tell me enough to prevent me from misjudging either you or Mr. Dare."

"You could not judge him too harshly!" he exclaimed,—broke off abruptly, and continued with restraint,—"a long story has led to my hostility, and one that I shall not permit myself to tell. You must guess from the way in which I lost my head at the sight of him, that the wrong he has done me is beyond pardon."

He hesitated, and his troubled eyes grew gravely grateful.

"Your touch on my hand brought many things to my remembrance, which I am ashamed that I forgot for a moment, — my duty here, whose chief object is to support such peace and order as is possible in Silverton; the certainty that if I attacked him the crowd would have flung itself at the throats of our party, and of the half a dozen troopers who would have sought to aid us."

Edith shivered involuntarily, and his eyes softened yet more.

"It was a danger from which you saved us, and which shall not occur again," he went on. "I am here to protect the charge intrusted to me, not to avenge my private feud. Nor is the wrong he did me punishable by law even if law existed here. For the present"— his breath came hurriedly as if the weight of his resolve oppressed him physically — "I shall merely watch him. According to general testimony he is doing work in the town which is desperately needed. So long as his influence is used to such good result, I shall neither say nor do anything to interfere with him there."

He stepped nearer her, and held out his hand.

"Will you forgive me that I alarmed you yesterday, and have made you uncomfortable this morning?" he asked.

"There is nothing to forgive," she said gently. "I am sorry that you must begin your stay at Ludlow with such a painful experience."

"Good gracious, Major Cornish!" Dorothy's voice cried from the doorway. "Did that wretched Ryan let you into this confusion?"

Cornish relinquished Edith's fingers, and greeted his hostess with perfunctory cheeriness.

"I have been making my excuses for leaving the riding party last night," he said.

"What are they?"

"Out-of-door preachings are not to my

liking," he replied, picking up his cap. "Though I admit that they produce admirable effects among certain classes, and this man appeared able to keep his audience."

" With one exception ! "

" With one exception," he repeated, slightly smiling. " Thank you again, Miss Lorimer. Good morning."

" I am afraid I was inopportune ! " Dorothy laughed when he was gone. " Has he not reached the hand-pressing era rather speedily ? "

"Nonsense ! " Edith answered lightly as she resumed her gloves and duster. " We were neither of us sentimental, I assure you ! In fact I have a humiliating suspicion that he did n't know he was holding my hand longer than formality required."

Despite her assumption of carelessness, however, Edith's thoughts were possessed by this interview with Cornish and divided into factions whose irreconcilabilities perplexed her. She was aware that a wide stride had been made in her esteem by this soldier who, because of the duty he owed to his position, could sternly repress the passionate enmity which had nearly overmastered him. She decided with a glow of enthusiasm that there was no more ennobling ideal than the soldierly one which, through all the world's history, has put self second to duty with such unhesitating directness as makes it matter-of-course to their profession. Yet in the midst of her enthusiasm she was convinced that Cornish judged his enemy harshly. The wrong which lay between them, and which the law could not punish, had been done to love, or ambition, or fortune, after such manner as to leave Dare comparatively blameless to any eyes but those of the man who had suffered. She would not try to guess the story, since a woman's knowledge covered scant distance in the lives of men. She would be content to admire the generosity of the enemy who withheld an influence which might have been potently adverse, without believing evil of the other whose daily life evidenced so great a power for good.

At this point in her meditations she anxiously remembered Dare's intention to seek Cornish this morning. Dorothy's entrance had prevented her from warning Cornish of the meeting which lay before him, and she was not altogether reassured by the reflection that both men appeared resolved to maintain the secret of their mutual antagonism.

The luncheon hour, which would bring her brother with a bulletin of garrison news, seemed long delayed. She was watching for him, between the curtains of the drawing-room windows, when he passed with Dare, and she presently heard his voice from the hall.

"At least come in and have something to drink? You must not carry away false impressions of Ludlow hospitality."

"Nothing to drink, thank you," Dare replied. "But I will come in for a moment to pull myself together! I find that, as a man grows older, he does not get into a rage with impunity."

Tom's laugh had an echo of embarrassment, and he perceived Edith with obvious relief.

"Here is my sister, who will regret as much as I that our plan has fallen through."

"The plan for the preaching?" she asked eagerly. "Why?"

"Major Cornish refuses his consent," Dare answered without formal greeting to her, and, sinking into an armchair, he leaned his elbow on his knee and his head on his hand.

Edith stood dumb with disappointment at this failure of Cornish's resolution, and with compassion for the enemy whose peace offering had evidently been roughly repulsed.

"Come, come, Dare," Tom said kindly. "Don't take this to heart! The troopers will rush to hear you in Silverton, if they suspect disapprobation at headquarters."

Dare lifted his head.

"He is pleased to declare that he will not interfere with my work in the town," he cried. "I wish he would try! He would stir up a hornet's nest capable of assailing even the commanding officer at Ludlow!"

"Be reasonable," Tom urged. "You know many excellent people only approve of religion when it is administered according to established forms and in consecrated buildings."

"If we should wait until we could provide the building, and the bishop for its consecration, how many of the men and women who come to my preaching would we get into a church?" Dare demanded vehemently.

"My dear fellow"—

"The sermons which have accomplished the most for the world's gain — from the Sermon on the Mount to Peter the Hermit, to John Wesley — were they not preached at the wayside?"

"Major Cornish's prejudices"—

"Major Cornish's hostility," Dare interrupted. "Though I have promised him to be silent in public as to the cause of his refusal, I am not bound to create a false impression with you. We are old acquaintances and old enemies."

He rose. He had regained his composure, and a grave grace which seemed habitual to him.

"Mere opposition or prejudice would neither have angered nor shaken me," he said. "They are to be expected and conquered in the life I lead. But when a man has set his feet on the right path, it hurts him to find barriers and stumbling-blocks built up against him out of the mistakes and misdeeds which he most bitterly repents."

He paused an instant, during which Tom and Edith made no reply.

"Major Cornish will not interfere with me in Silverton, and I am not to intrude upon him here," Dare continued. "It is an armed truce which he permits! Lamentations are as weak as they are useless, but — I had hoped and prayed for peace."

His voice trembled on the last word.

She knew so much good of him that she would not suspect evil, Edith told her half indignant, half sympathetic heart. This moment of his evident discouragement was most suitable for an assurance of support, and an announcement of the plan she had cherished ever since her coming to Ludlow; while, now that Major Cornish's favor was hopeless, the struggle to win Tom's consent would be equally sharp, either at present or in the future.

"Will you give me something to do for your work, Mr. Dare?" she exclaimed impetuously. "I am very idle, and, Tom dear, — very lonely! There must be poor women I can help or children I can teach."

"Edith, I could not allow — "

"Tom, it is such work as our father allowed in New York."

"New York isn't Silverton. Tell her, Dare, that it is impossible!"

"Why is it impossible?" Dare asked gently, looking from brother to sister with comprehending swiftness. "Miss Lorimer, I thank you more than I can say, and I will only avail myself of your goodness in some way to which your brother need not object. Will you trust me, Captain, in spite of your commanding officer?"

"I will reserve my answer until I hear what you propose for my sister," Tom declared brusquely; but Edith's smile promised fullest confidence.

"Thank you both," Dare said vigorously. "My first visit to Ludlow will prove happy after all!"

"I hope you will come again to see Mrs. Lorimer," Tom exclaimed, his hospitable soul finding ill-humor untenable toward a departing guest. He followed Dare to the hall door, and returned to confront Edith.

"Now, Miss Lorimer," he demanded, "what mischief do you desire?"

She laid a pretty hand on each of his shoulders, and smiled.

"Mischief is for idleness," she asserted. "I ask for work."

"You will never get my consent to running about that den of iniquity! Remember 'charity begins at home,' and that you can find scope for your energies in 'laundress-row.'"

He pinched her cheek and walked away, but came back immediately.

"There is no need to start gossip concerning an old hostility as the reason that Dare has been refused permission to preach here. The Major was wise to wish it assigned to religious prejudice, and I'll wager Dare is already regretting that his anger led him into this confession."

"I thought Major Cornish superior to such tyranny."

"My dear girl, we don't know what occurred in their past, and we cannot judge of it," he said gravely. "The Major's record is one of which the army is proud, and Dare is making a noble effort in Silverton. We owe it to them, and to the best interests of the post and the town, to refrain from widening any breach between them. I shall not even tell Dorothy!"

The seal of solemnity which he evidently considered that this final assurance put upon his purpose amused his sister. But she was glad to be silent on a subject which had disappointed her as regarded Cornish, and inspired some unwilling doubts of Dare.

She remained silent even under the temptation of Mrs. Blount's unexpected approbation of the commanding officer's religious scruples.

"It sounds narrow at first hearing," that volatile lady admitted. "But, in these lax days, it is admirable to find a man so convinced that only his own church is right."

"Not so!" Edith exclaimed. "If Dr. Blount had a patient whom he failed to cure he would consent to call in another doctor! Why should we be less insistent when souls are to be saved instead of bodies?"

"Silverton may require homeopathic, or other irregular practice," Mrs. Blount responded, laughing. "But we are in no such extreme case, even though we have not been provided with an orthodox chaplain. According to all accounts the troopers are very decent fellows; and as for 'officers'-row,' its inhabitants are as nearly saints as an entire lack of temptation to be anything else can make them!"

She departed, and Edith betook herself to the piano. Her playing was apt to lapse into memories, more sympathetic than technically correct, of music which haunted her thoughts, and to give greater pleasure to a listener who was not a musician than would a brilliantly accurate performance.

Cornish, after lingering for an instant outside the windows, entered the hospitably open doorway.

At the sound of a footstep Edith glanced across her shoulder, and rose.

"Please go on," he said. "I had a feeling that I was eavesdropping while listening without your knowledge! But I hoped that you would let me hear more if I confessed my presence?"

"I don't think I can," she answered lightly. "An audience scatters my recollections!"

He made no entreaty; entreaties, she fancied, were not in his line, and this was a subject on which he could scarcely command, even at Ludlow!

"My sister and brother have gone for a ride," she added, to fill the pause of his silence.

"A fact which is also to blame for my intrusion," he said, smiling. "I am not usually inclined to talk about myself, yet I seem most inconsistently desirous to do so with you."

"That is nice of you!"

His smile vanished.

"You have been told my decision concerning the preaching to the troops," he continued earnestly. "And you think it a deviation from the course I had resolved upon with regard to this — Dare?"

"I am disappointed," she replied coldly. "I thought you magnanimous, and you force me to find you ungenerous."

Cornish leaned back in his chair, and gazed wordlessly through the open window during a long moment.

"Putting aside such ornamental terms as magnanimity and generosity," he said at last, "it appears to me understandable that, though I abstain from interference with an influence which is accomplishing an undeniable good at Silverton, I should not consider myself justified in ordering my troops to receive religious instruction from a man whom I know to be a scoundrel, — and whom I suspect to be using a fanatical oratory as a means of personal aggrandizement."

"Do you consider yourself justified in thus accusing him, without proving your accusation?" Edith exclaimed, while her bright eyes appealed against his arbitrariness yet more indignantly than her words.

His glance met hers fixedly, and he flushed slowly over all his resolute bronzed countenance.

"I do not accuse him, except to you," he murmured.

"I wish you would not except me," she answered impatiently. "Of course, circumstances have rather compelled you to do so. But I dislike half measures, half confidences — they are as bewildering as half lights."

His glance drooped. He frowned.

"You are right," he said. "I ask too much of your slight knowledge of me. Only an old friend could justify me without evidence and, though I possess that evidence, I — I — " he broke off with a nervous laugh.

"If speech were suddenly given to a man who had been dumb for years, cannot you imagine that it would be difficult for him?" he went on rapidly. "Though we are almost strangers, I should like to tell you a story which would gain your sympathy for me; yet — some day — perhaps" —

He rose.

"Shall we make a new beginning, with one subject left out between us, — for the present?"

Edith was aware of a swift desire to detain him.

"Here is my hand for peace — not for good-by," she exclaimed with a smile, which a pang of self-reproach softened wondrously. "You have had a monopoly of amiability so far at this interview! I have disputed you, and criticised and rebuked you, for a quarter of an hour. Now let me confess that you deserve something better, and, as the best I can give is my singing, let me bestow some of it upon you immediately."

When Tom and Dorothy returned Cornish had not departed. Nor did he hesitate to accept their invitation to dinner with the same cheerful informality with which it was offered.

Maiden meditation is mostly occupied in our generation with self analysis. Indeed, as "the human heart changeth not," it has probably been so occupied since the world began. Edith had forbidden her thoughts to question the manner in which the lives of these two men had crossed each other, beyond the obvious certainty that Cornish held himself wronged and that Dare declared himself misjudged. The question she confronted in her own room that night concerned her compact to help Dare with his work at Silverton. How was it that she had made no mention of this compact in entering upon her treaty of friendship with Cornish? It was not a lack of frankness of which she finally remained accused, but an entire forgetfulness.

What had caused this forgetfulness of a plan which had been dear to her for several weeks?

What made the certainty that Dare would promptly provide work for her less attractive than when she had asked him for it?

Edith's heart beat faster as she heard again the low hurried voice which confessed that a dumb spirit struggled to find words to claim her sympathy.

Would Cornish be hurt by a doubt of her sincerity, when he knew that she was pledged to give assistance to Dare? She grew restlessly desirous that some chance of garrison propinquity should bring them together, that she might tell him of her purpose, in such manner as not to wound a nature which she had divined to be as sensitive as it was reserved.

During the succeeding days Cornish, however, frustrated this desire by his devotion to the business which necessarily attends the installation of a post-commander and the transfer of the reins of authority to new hands.

Very vigorous hands his subordinates considered them.

His predecessor had been lax in many ways. The number of inspections, extra drills, and stern brief lectures which Cornish administered during the fortnight succeeding his arrival did not tend to his popularity, though they produced a perceptible improvement in military routine.

This result Tom Lorimer admitted with dolorous approbation to his home circle.

"We were getting slack and untidy under dear old Wharton," he said ruefully. "But by Jove! this fellow means to keep us as perpetually on the jump as though the general-in-chief — or all the redskins of the department — were coming down upon us to-morrow!"

"I saw him riding to quarters just before dinner, so gray with dust that only memory told me his uniform must be blue, in spite of appearances!" Edith laughed.

"He had been putting Troop E through its paces out on the prairie. His sentiments concerning their drill this morning made Jackson hotter than the weather! But Cornish is all right," Tom concluded briskly. "Though the men swear at him now, they will swear by him presently! Soldiers should be added to that wise proverb, 'A woman, a spaniel, and a willow tree, the harder you treat them the better they be.' Eh, Dolly?"

The next afternoon Mrs. Blount, Dorothy, and Edith were loitering over five-o'clock tea, when in the doorway, open to the chance of a breeze, there stood the picturesque figure of Dare; so picturesque, indeed, was he in the cow-boy dress, which makes most men merely slovenly, that Edith asked herself whether his perception of that fact did not induce his adoption of it. For, despite her conviction of his sincerity, and her respect for his earnestness, she had at her last meeting with him perceived a certain content in the effectiveness of his pose.

"We are very glad to see you, Mr. Dare," Dorothy exclaimed, with the cordial frontier hospitality which her natural graciousness and Tom's wishes had rendered easy to her acquirement. "There is a comfortable chair, and here is a cup of tea. Or you can have it with ice and rum if you will wait an instant."

He accepted the tea in its orthodox combination, and agreed to the lamentations on the heat of the weather.

"The Northwest does everything thoroughly," he said with a brief brilliant smile. "I have an errand, however, from which I hope such good results that no vagary of the thermometer could spoil my pleasure!"

He looked at Edith as he spoke, and she interpreted his glance.

"You have found something for me to do? I am very glad!"

Was she very glad in truth? Or did her conscience declare that she should be so?

"Thank you," Dare continued. "I have an urgent need in which your help will be exceedingly valuable."

"Something for my sister to do in the town?" Dorothy asked. "I fear that Captain Lorimer" —

"Tom knows, Dolly dear, that I begged Mr. Dare to find work for me at Silverton," Edith interposed hastily. "I think he will not be quite irreconcilable after a little coaxing."

"You shall admit the harmlessness of my plan when I have explained it," Dare exclaimed. "We have all of us heard that much of the influence of the 'Moody revivals' is due to Sankey's choir. Such similar services as I am endeavoring to establish at Silverton should also be accompanied by singing"—

"My husband will never consent that Edith should sing before a Silverton crowd!" Dorothy interrupted, while Edith remembered those rows of upturned faces which the moonlight had spiritualized without softening, and wondered whether their confronting would appall or inspire her.

"I do not ask that ordeal of Miss Lorimer," Dare replied; "I beg her to teach a dozen young men and women to render God's service more attractive to their fellow creatures."

A strong patience possessed his look and voice, which moved Edith to forgetfulness of everything but her long-desired work.

"I am eager and happy to teach them!" she cried. "Can they come to me, or shall I go to them?"

With few words he detailed his arrangement that her class should meet her two or three times each week, on any days she chose and at the house of the manager of the "Yankee Doodle mine."

"His wife in her own rank is as conventional, yet as devoutly subject to higher creeds, as any lady at Ludlow," Dare concluded, smiling.

"May I come too?" Mrs. Blount implored, her erratic sympathy again on the wing. "I can play for the singers, and Captain Lorimer will be easily reconciled to your project if Edith is properly chaperoned."

Dare accepted gratefully and, as he rose to leave, Tom entered and received with slight opposition the announcement of their intentions.

"The manager of the 'Yankee Doodle' is an excellent chap," he said. "Therefore his wife"—

"Must be an excellent chap also," Mrs. Blount laughed.

"It is work which will bring these ladies in contact with nothing unpleasant," Dare asserted.

"It is work of which we are capable," Edith added. "Consent nicely, Tom dear, because if you do not"—

"You will plant a red flag on the barricades," Tom exclaimed gayly. "If Dr. Blount"—

"I'll answer for Dr. Blount," cried that gentleman's "active partner."

"I yield! The responsibility is yours, Dare," Tom declared. Then he drew himself erect with mock stateliness. "Know, ladies, that you have threatened your commanding officer with revolt."

There ensued a chorus of questions.

"Much against his will Cornish has gone to take part in a court-martial at Department Headquarters."

"The poor troopers will have a little rest," Mrs. Blount said rejoicingly.

"Do you fancy I intend to be a sluggard?" Tom inquired.

"You didn't overwork them before Major Cornish came."

"He has converted me to energy, — and converts are more zealous than those who have never been sinners — eh, Dare?"

"Why do you ask me?"

"Why?" repeated the surprised Tom. "Converts and sinners suggest religious revivals, and you" —

"I beg your pardon," Dare interrupted, coloring hotly. "I scarcely heard what you were saying."

Thereupon he took his leave somewhat hurriedly, after receiving promises from Edith and Mrs. Blount that they would meet the singing class on the following day.

"There is a history and a mystery," Tom exclaimed, shrugging his shoulders.

"Just what we women had already divined," Mrs. Blount said, laughing. "We knew at first sight that Mr. Dare's handsome eyes did not derive all their power of expression from a life of unvaried saintliness."

"I wish that Cornish were here," Tom said meditatively when Mrs. Blount was gone. "He would feel bound to tell me if there is anything in that fellow's past which should prevent me from trusting my womenkind to his acquaintance."

"You decided that we must judge Mr. Dare by his present," Edith replied resolutely. "Nobody could shrink from the task he has assigned us, and he is so busy that I doubt if we see him at the singing lessons."

Tom whistled cynically, but she wisely declined this fraternal challenge, and left the room.

The next afternoon was of ideal summer weather. A thunder storm during the night had cooled the air and laid the dust, and the radiant sunshine was not too hot.

Dr. Blount rode over to Silverton with the two ladies and consigned them to the hospitality of Mrs. Brown, the manager's wife, with a promise to call for them in an hour. They found their class intelligent, decorous, and possessing a couple of voices whose possibilities filled the amateur teachers with enthusiasm. When future meetings had been fixed, and the class dispersed, Mrs. Brown besought Mrs. Blount and Edith to take a cup of tea, and, though Dr. Blount had reappeared, it seemed unkindly to refuse. The cup of tea developed, according to the fashion of their hostess' social sphere, into a substantial repast, spread in a dining-room which was the pride of its owner's heart, and made as glittering a display of inlaid wood and gilded monograms as though it had been a palace car.

Mrs. Brown's conversation, however, rewarded her guests' amiability, being composed chiefly of personal anecdotes concerning Dare. None of these stories antedated his arrival at Silverton. Yet misgivings as to the past which preceded such a present as they proved, seemed untenable even to the shrewd elderly surgeon. Practical helpfulness and tireless religious zeal mingled in these stories. But there were also adventures where fearless courage had done even more to capture the hearts of the tumultuous vassals whose sovereign he had undoubtedly become.

"Nobody will forget what he did when them 'Spread Eagle' boys got into that fix through bad management," Mrs. Brown said, waving aside Dr. Blount's reference to Dare's début in the settlement.

Like some arbitrary hostesses in more fashionable circles, she intended to entertain her guests herself, — and, though her grammar was fantastic, her style of narrative was not without a force lacking in discourses of greater polish.

"Dare showed his make when he volunteered to lead them into that fiery pit," she continued. "But he has given us many a token that he rates his life cheap beside a neighbor's need of help, — which is a tighter 'cinch' on the town than his preachings, or his club, or any of his schemes, though they do a lot of good, too."

"Tell us some of his exploits," cried Mrs. Blount, and no other urging was required.

"It is maybe six weeks," she began, noisily stirring her third cup of tea. "Young Frost, who is son to the boss ranchman of —— County, he came down here with a lot of cattle to ship East. He is a handsome, merry chap that his father has kept pretty strict mostly. This trip, however, the old man was forty miles away, and the boy, with his pockets full of money, 'fell among thieves' — as the Bible says! Poker and bad whiskey all night and all day made him soon fit to paint the town red. I had been over to Dare's store, and was walking home one forenoon, when I heard pistol shots from Simpson's saloon, and out bundled half a dozen men. They did n't go no further than the sidewalk. Some of them stood there laughing rather shamefaced, and some of them peeped into the big window and reported proceedings. The shots went on popping briskly inside, and, as I got closer, Dare passed me on the run."

"Did you go near the shooting?" Mrs. Blount exclaimed, aghast.

"I've been a good bit nearer," Mrs. Brown answered grimly. "Lord, ladies! You belong to the army, where they keep their women folks away from the smell of powder, but we frontiersmen's wives, we get used to it! I heard Dare ask what was up. 'Young Frost crazy drunk,' somebody sang out; 'swore he would empty Simpson's place single-handed and has done it too' — 'Except Simpson,' somebody else chuckled. 'Where is he?' says Dare. — 'Under the bar.' — 'Hurt?' — 'Not unless with broken glass! He went for cover when Frost's first bullet smashed the big mirror behind his stand.' Dare walked to the door. 'See here, preacher,' a tall fellow shouted, 'he is dangerous. Let him alone and he will quiet off directly.' 'With a bullet in his head,' Dare cried, facing them, and I tell you, ladies, he looked fine! 'That is the way things quieted off the last time you drove a lad out of his wits with your devil's tricks! Stand back!' he called aloud and clear. 'I 'm going in!' and in he went. Well! the Almighty takes care of his own sometimes! Frost fired straight at him, missed him, and with a rush Dare knocked up the revolver. Then, as they grappled, the poor boy fainted in Dare's arms, and the play was over."

" As plucky a thing as ever I heard," Dr. Blount exclaimed, while his wife wiped her eyes.

"What did Mr. Dare do with young Frost?" Edith asked, her low voice thrilling.

"Ah! you guessed he was n't likely to leave him half saved, eh?" Mrs. Brown cried delightedly. "He helped to carry him to his own place, nursed him through a sharp touch of fever, and sent him home to the ranch with a lesson the young fellow will be the better for as long as he lives. Those are what Dare calls his 'opportunities,'" she concluded, while her guests rose to go, "nor he don't lose any!"

This story Edith promptly repeated to her brother, and when added to the fact that Dare had not presented himself at the singing lesson, it accomplished much toward soothing Tom's dislike for an enterprise which progressed amazingly during six or seven meetings.

The fortnight of Cornish's intended absence at the court martial lapsed into a third week before Tom received a telegram announcing his return on a certain evening.

It was an exceedingly hot day, and one appointed for the class at Silverton. Mrs. Blount discovered sufficient headache to absolve her from a shadeless ride which had lost its charm of novelty, but her good-natured husband escorted Edith as usual.

She had ceased to expect Dare's presence on these occasions, and was surprised to find him at Mrs. Brown's that afternoon. Nothing, however, could be more natural than his desire to judge how soon her pupils might appear at his preachings. He listened with interest, praised gratefully and discriminatingly, and, when the class dispersed, accepted Mrs. Brown's invitation to tea.

"I am glad she induced you to stay," Edith said, as their hostess vanished, " on hospitable thought intent." " You look overworked, and one should spare one's strength in such hot weather as this."

" I am not tired," Dare replied. " I am anxious and annoyed."

" May I know why? My concern for your efforts here is very sincere."

"It is my wish to tell you,—if Mrs. Brown spares us time," he said with a fleeting smile. "I have heard that Major Cornish returns to-night," he went on after a moment's pause, during which he grew visibly paler.

"You are ill," she exclaimed. "Let me call"—

"Do you understand what a panic means? A chill which shivers with exaggerated apprehension? That is what ails me." Dare had begun to speak haltingly, but he continued rapidly. "Do you remember the terms of the truce between Major Cornish and me? He would not interfere with me here, and I must not intrude upon him at Ludlow. He will consider the assistance I receive from the ladies of the post as an infringement of our compact. He will so tell the story of our enmity to your brother as to induce you to break off your work."

Edith's color had faded also.

"What I do will depend, of course, upon the story," she said coldly.

"Every story varies with the bias of the person who tells it," he exclaimed, a curious cynicism piercing his earnestness. "I wish to anticipate him, if you will hear me."

He broke off as Mrs. Brown's stout figure appeared.

"My good friend," he said gently, "I have something of importance to say to Miss Lorimer. I am sure you will not mind if I ask you to leave us alone for a few moments?"

"Why, no, indeed!" his hearty admirer responded. "Whatever you say goes, Mr. Dare! Just step out when you get ready, and you will find I've kept your tea nice for you both."

Dare walked restlessly the length of the room.

"It is like tearing bandages from a wound to speak of these things," he muttered, dropping into a chair beside Edith.

"Must you speak of them?"

"Either he or I."

"Major Cornish would deal fairly"—

"He could not! I have cost him too dear."

There was silence.

"We were boys together," he began in low tones, which expressed chiefly haste to end his task. "We were chums who shared each other's pleasures and fought each other's battles. At seventeen we left school. He went to West Point, and I went — as near destruction as a boy more mad than bad could go. Chance threw us together again when he was on his way home for long leave after graduating. He was triumphant with success and bright prospects. I was reckless, with no prospect but ruin! He took me to his home, and kept the worst of my exploits from his mother and sister. His sister" —

Dare's voice sank quite away.

"Don't tell me," she murmured. "Trust us not to judge you harshly."

"I wish Major Cornish to know that I do not claim your friendship under false pretenses," he answered.

He leaned his elbows on his knees, his head on his clasped hands, and with his face thus partially hidden, he continued the story.

"Rosamond was eighteen. She was on the verge of a marriage which her mother urged, and to which she had been dutifully influenced. From the day we met that marriage became impossible. It was equally impossible to take either her mother or Cornish into our confidence. At the first word of our love I should have been banished, and even letters forbidden between us. After long hesitation, I persuaded her to run away with me. We were married. Rosamond wrote to her mother, imploring pardon. It was offered to her if she would give up her husband. My wife refused. Some little money she possessed was sent to her, and the correspondence ceased. We went to Texas, and bought a ranch. Things got wrong with us at once. God knows I do not deny that all was my fault! We quarreled. I left her much alone. Our child died while I was absent. When I returned she had gone, leaving a letter which swore that I should never see her again. She kept her word. Five years later, a clergyman wrote me that she was dead. He forwarded a message of pardon for me, a prayer to live so that we may meet hereafter, and a small sum she had saved by teaching in a mission school."

The short, tense sentences ended. Dare lifted his head and confronted Edith.

"That is my story, for which my own unforgiveness is sterner than Cornish's can be. Yet it shall not stand between me and the use to which I have dedicated such days as remain to me."

He sprang to his feet. His pale face flushed. A light burned in his eyes, as when he preached to listening Silverton.

"My wife, whose heart I broke, forgave me. The Lord my God, against whom I have greatly sinned, will not withhold his pardon from my repentance. What are this man's wrongs that he should cherish his wrath and his hope for my defeat, though I have humbled myself to him? — I will make that wrath and that hope vain!" he broke off sharply. "Will you too turn aside from a sinner who asks only that his penitence may be allowed to work for the good of others?"

Edith answered mutely with her tears. There was a tap of Dr. Blount's whip-handle on the door. Dare recovered his composure instantly. She drew down her veil, and the surgeon observed nothing.

But Mrs. Brown's tea party was less cheerily prolonged than that excellent woman's hospitality desired.

When Dare lifted Edith to her saddle, she met his sombre eyes frankly.

"I shall come on Thursday, — storm or shine," she said.

Thus she unfurled her standard, and resolved that she would defend it.

Dr. Blount, as happens with the husbands of talkative wives, was inclined to silence, and, during their homeward ride, Edith filled the gaps in Dare's story with many imaginings.

The figure of that proud Rosamond who loved faithfully and resented bitterly was intensely present to her. She could fancy the sister's likeness to the brother; for Cornish might be yet more unrelenting to a love which had failed him than to a hatred which he believed justified.

Edith's heart grew very tender toward this woman, too stern to pardon when the limit she set for pardon was passed, too loyal to go home to the welcome which awaited her return alone, — but through all those years of absence loving her husband, toiling for him, yearning for him even in death.

And Dare? — if he had sinned he had suffered and repented. Surely no repentance could be better proved than this, confessed with such anguish, and whose results were uplifting a whole community day by day.

Yet Cornish would not accept this proof!

He had called it a scheme for self-aggrandizement.

Ah, well! The friend whose trust had been betrayed, the brother who knew that his sister's life had been blighted, must find forgiveness bitterly difficult. Would that dumb spirit which possessed him permit him to tell her his version of the story when she next saw him?

She would be true to both these men who had asked for her friendship; if, through her mediation, they should come to a reconciliation, that might be a work to thank God for bestowing upon her.

III

THAT evening at dinner Tom Lorimer announced Cornish's return.

"By Jove," he declared complacently, "we must be a pleasanter set than I thought, for he is unmistakably glad to get back to us."

"He likes his work, I daresay," Edith suggested.

"No, he had not the manner of a fellow settling to congenial tasks. His interest in the post gossip was like a home-coming,"—a statement with which Edith was content, though she abstained from asking herself, after her usual introspective fashion, the value to her of Major Cornish's satisfaction in his return to Ludlow.

On the following morning a letter from Dare was brought to her at the breakfast table,—a letter which so startled her, that with effort she was barely able to avoid attracting attention from Tom or Dorothy.

"I intended yesterday to tell you merely such details of my past life as produced Major Cornish's hostility to me. The five years which elapsed between my wife's flight and her death have no connection with this hostility, and I spared myself the pain of shocking you yet further. I feel now, however, that I have been unfair in appearing to confess to you all that might prejudice you, without acknowledging so black a stain as I concealed from you. During those five years I was a convict at the Texas State Penitentiary, to which I had been condemned for shooting a man in a gambling fight, soon after my wife left me, — a deed for whose poor excuse I can say that it was done in self-defense. This sentence seemed on its imposition so terrible a consummation of my debasement that I did not willingly survive it. Yet this sentence proved to be the mercy of my God. Broken in mind and body, I came under the influence of the chaplain, whose blessed teaching brought to me the one remedy for my despair, while those years of regular labor and restraint restored me to the physical vigor needed for the purpose with which he inspired me. Several months of my term were remitted to me for good conduct on the same day that I was told of my wife's death. That was two years since, and I joined a mission at a mining town in Pennsylvania, where I worked until I was considered fit to go on without direction. Then I came here. I hope that the loyalty of those who believe in my work here will remain unshaken, even if the story of my sins and their punishment is made public; sinners are more convinced of the force of repentance than those who have less erred. But to lose your sympathy and your brother's will be a grief to me, — and I should have my hands strengthened for the warfare I wage daily, by all who wish that cause well. DARE.

"My name is Darrell, and the change was owing to the advice of those whom I am bound to consult, but I have always been ready to encounter the consequences of recognition."

The morning passed to Edith as in a dream. She was shocked through every instinctive aversion. Yet she was aware that she meant to defend yesterday's resolve, though it would assuredly be opposed by those who had a right to seek to influence her.

Her belief in Dare's sincerity was unshaken.

Why then should she shrink aside from him because he admitted himself to be a greater sinner? Were there not sinners among those who, following the steps of Jesus of Nazareth, became the saints whose life and death do yet benefit the world?

Was not Dare's repentance also bearing visible fruit?

With a pang she had no need to analyze she decided to resist any adverse influence which Cornish might exert upon Tom, and, though she dreaded the struggle, she knew that she should find courage when required. Nor was she mistaken.

Tom returned to luncheon severe of mien, and summoned her to an interview in his particular sanctum. Cornish, having heard of Mrs. Blount's and Miss Lorimer's visits to the singing class at Silverton, had repeated briefly to their masculine protectors the chief facts of Dare's story. Tom reported that he had done this with such obvious dislike to the task as showed that only a sense of duty had compelled him to speak of his sister's sorrows.

Tom's verdict was that a civil note must be written to Dare, explaining that, for various reasons, the ladies found it impossible to continue their instruction to the singing class.

With a flutter at her throat Edith flung down her gage of battle.

"Mr. Dare told me the whole story," she said slowly. "It is one of the saddest that can be imagined, and one which Major Cornish cannot judge dispassionately. But, knowing what we do of Mr. Dare's life at Silverton, I see no reason why I should give up a good work merely because he directed me to it."

"Are you mad, Edith?" Tom exclaimed. "A man-slayer, an ex-convict! — Those are facts which Cornish's resentment does not blacken."

"Between us and those facts of the past stands a present whose influence I have heard you praise."

"I admire it heartily. Even Cornish admits that his position requires formal public consideration from us, and privately I shall continue to meet him as though I had never heard this story. But a reformed scapegrace, whose zeal and abilities may be valuable at Silverton, is not necessarily a fit associate for my sister."

"I have promised to prepare this choir for him."

"You can write him that I have withdrawn my consent."

"That would be a pretext whose real meaning he could readily guess."

"Let him guess!"

"No, Tom, I am pledged to my self-respect for my own word, which I gave freely."

Tom lost his temper.

"I daresay you would be less obstinate if this adventurer had a squint or a snub nose!"

"Tom!"

"That is what our friends will say."

"You should not set them the example!"

With which she made an exit in good order, for Tom was already ashamed of having displayed an anxiety which he intended to keep to himself.

Edith's battle, however, was only begun. Dorothy invaded her retreat with tearful petitions against vexing Tom in a case where he was so clearly right, as if there could be any imaginable case, that did not concern the management of Baby, where she would consider him wrong! Later, too, Mrs. Blount appeared, full of enjoyable chatter over a crisis which relieved the dullness of Ludlow, and divided between delight at the idea of rebelling from the lawful authorities, and amused dismay at the suggestion of taking part with an ex-convict.

This half-hearted support, the strenuous opposition of the others, and the vague misgiving of which she was herself conscious, rendered Edith's day long and weary. After dinner, to escape the tacit reproach of her brother's gloomy countenance, she walked through the windows of the drawing-room to a veranda which extended the length of "officers'-row," and overlooked the ramparts. The commandant's quarters were two doors beyond Captain Lorimer's, and, as she sank into a low wicker chair, she saw Cornish lounging outside his own domain.

He threw away his cigar and came toward her.

"Good-evening," he said alertly. "May I make you a visit here?"

She laid her hand assentingly on the chair beside her.

"My brother says that you are glad to get back to Ludlow in spite of our dullness?"

"Very glad! The court martial was a business we were all pleased to conclude."

"Whose case was it?"

"Captain Watson's of the ——th Cavalry. An excellent record he had until garrison idleness ruined him."

"What was the result?"

"Acquittal on the worst charge, which concerned a confusion in his troop accounts, and a severe reprimand for various lesser misdoings. But he will resign, poor old chap, that is understood."

"You were sorry for him?"

"So was every one, except the Judge Advocate! He, fortunately, became entangled in his own 'red-tape,' and we got poor Watson off while he was extricating himself."

"And you were sorry for Captain Watson? You wanted him to escape humiliation?"

"Why not? He has done firstrate field service"— Cornish paused. The meaning of her reproachful gaze flashed upon him, and the lines of his face grew harder.

"There can be no comparison between Captain Watson's case and that of Mr. — Dare."

"None, except in the disproportion of your sympathy! The cause of my friend rests on higher claims than yours can make. Mine is daily proving the strenuousness of his self-conquest. Yours struggles merely to avoid the consequences of his misdeeds."

"Do not call him your friend!" Cornish exclaimed.

"He is my friend, in so far that I believe his sincere repentance, and that I honor the mission he is accomplishing here," she declared earnestly. "When he told me his story" —

"He has told it to you?"

"Even you would have softened to him, could you have heard him."

"I soften to him!" Cornish repeated bitterly. "It required all my certainty of the fatal consequences of a row between the chief authorities here and at Silverton to keep my hands from his throat when he tried his dramatic narrative on me."

"I feel how unpardonable he must seem to you," she murmured. "He accused himself of breaking your sister's heart."

"Picturesque confession! But the details were not artistic. He left her alone with a sick child and a besotted Chinese servant. The child grew worse. My sister rode twenty miles, with the child in her arms, to find a doctor. The child died an hour after she reached the town, — while her husband was raving at a tavern after a week's excess. These particulars I learned from her acquaintances there, when I went to Texas to search for her after he was sent to prison for manslaughter."

"She forgave him before she died."

"She did not know that which she would never have forgiven him — or herself." Cornish's voice quivered. "My mother was found dead, — holding a newspaper in which she had read the announcement of his sentence to the penitentiary, and that no clue could be discovered to the whereabouts of his young wife, who had fled from his ill treatment a few weeks previously."

He averted his face, and there was silence.

Presently Edith leaned forward, and very softly touched the brown hand which was clinched on the arm of his chair. His fingers closed over hers, but he neither spoke nor looked at her until she drew back. Then he turned and, with a pang both sharp and sweet, she saw the tears on his cheek.

"It seems wonderful — yet quite natural — that I should come to you with a grief of which I could never talk to any one," he murmured, his eyes meeting hers lingeringly.

This was the instant of supreme temptation for Edith's loyalty to the course on which she had determined. To repulse, ever so slightly, the half spontaneous, half involuntary confidence of Cornish, hurt her as though by so doing she risked losing something utterly her own and belonging to her inmost life. But the thought of the peace to which she might lead him succored her failing resolution.

"If he has no knowledge that your mother's death separates you thus cruelly"—she began after a little.

"You still defend him?"

"No, no! Not defend him!" she exclaimed — and the rising moon showed her fair vehemence. "It is for you I contend, — for the comfort to yourself if you can pardon him. Don't you know that the bitterness would go out of your grief for your dead, if you can believe that his life is a long remorse for the heartbreak he caused them?"

Cornish gazed dumbly away from her across the post ramparts, to the wide silvery stretches of sky and hillsides which lay beyond.

"Remember that, trusting his promises of reform, I forced all that came afterward upon them," he said at last, and the pain of the low, slow tones was unutterable. "I brought him as my friend to my mother's house."

"Surely you do not torture yourself with such an accusation?"

"But I do," he said gently. "If it is hard to forgive myself, it is impossible to forgive him — or to re-create a belief whose destruction cost me so dearly."

He rose.

"Please, please do not doubt my sympathy, my friendship for you, because I am sorry for him also," she cried with a little sob.

"No revelation of yourself could make me doubt you," he answered. "You are truth incarnate. But such perfect truth is easy to deceive."

With which he lifted her hand to his lips, and walked down the veranda to his quarters.

And Edith wondered vaguely in what dream, that had always been familiar, a man with shining eyes had so kissed her hand, while her whole being thrilled to his touch!

There ensued three or four days of tacit hostility between Edith and her family. She met Cornish only once, at a dinner given by Mrs. Blount, where he ably seconded her efforts to steer safely through the shoals and rapids of allusion to the singing class, whither their mischief-loving hostess continually led conversation.

The afternoon succeeding this dinner was that appointed for the next expedition to Silverton, and in the morning Mrs. Blount appeared to confess her capitulation to an assertion of marital authority. Moreover she declared her gradual conversion to the perception that Dare's antecedents, though not unfit preparation for his mission at Silverton, were scarcely suited to intimate association with the ladies of Ludlow. Like all renegades she was eager to proselyte, but Edith remained stanch. She admitted that Mrs. Blount's desertion crippled her facilities for going to the town. Yet she insisted that she must fulfill her promise to prepare the choir, — a work which she hoped to accomplish in a couple of additional meetings.

The immediate need was to find means of getting to the class that afternoon. Tom, being "officer of the day," was inaccessible either to coaxing or coercion, while Dr. Blount had of course become impossible, and, for some occult reason of the quartermaster, the ambulance was also forbidden.

Finally Edith wrote to Lieutenant Gwynne, with whom she often rode, asking him to accompany her to Silverton.

Thus it was arranged, and they set forth at the appointed hour.

Some accident to the machinery of the "Spread Eagle" mine had bestowed a holiday upon its employees. The long squalid street of the town was adorned by numerous groups of loafers, and Edith became promptly aware that a rumor of the opposition she had surmounted in coming to her class had been wafted to these grimy citizens. Nor did they hesitate from manifesting their approbation of herself and her object, as they understood them.

"She ain't afraid to stand up for those she likes, if she is a lady!" Such was the first remark intended for her hearing.

"She has got eyes to see that the best of them officer chaps ain't fit to black Dare's boots." This was the next individual utterance of general opinion.

Gwynne laughed confusedly, and she exclaimed: —

"Let us ride faster; I am afraid those men are drunk!"

One of them gave every sign of so being, for, as she spoke, he reeled forward, waving a battered cap.

"Three cheers for the preacher's sweetheart!" he shouted.

Edith flushed hotly, and Gwynne pulled in his horse — then with a wiser impulse urged him on again.

"The fool was crazy drunk! Not worth thrashing," he said deprecatingly a moment later, while he lifted her from the saddle before Mrs. Brown's door. "I should have made you more uncomfortable!"

"Of course," she assented vehemently. "It would be absurdly beneath us to resent such impertinence."

He promised to return for her at the end of an hour and left her.

To Edith's awakened perception of Silverton's hunger for romance, Mrs. Brown's greeting demonstrated a caressing comprehension which was offensive, and she detected a new element of gushing sentiment among her feminine pupils. Upon both these unwelcome manifestations she set an effectual blight by the cold announcement that this was her farewell lesson.

She had not indeed been aware of the definiteness of her decision until she felt compelled to declare it! But, when the class dispersed after a somewhat embarrassing leave-taking, she waited impatiently for the arrival of Dare, who had told Mrs. Brown to expect him. It would be possible to speak frankly to him of the whole situation, Edith thought. However both Ludlow and Silverton misread her motives, she was confident that he comprehended them.

She was right.

His dark eyes met her with a sincere regret which had no tincture of self-consciousness, when he entered presently.

"I am more vexed than I can say that you should have been annoyed," he exclaimed. "I knew that your faithful kindness would encounter opposition among your own people, but I never suspected that such a stupidity as this could have gained belief here! It is intolerable; I" —

"Please do nothing concerning it," Edith interrupted hurriedly. "Like any other form of gossip it will be made worse by treating it seriously."

"You will not abandon us?"

"The class can be ready for what you require of them, if you will give them a couple of rehearsals," she said, turning from his keen glance to the open window. "They have aptitude and zeal, and their progress justifies — What is that?" she broke off abruptly.

The sudden clamor which had startled her brought Dare to her side.

A curious alert expectancy pervaded the street. Various groups of passers had halted, and were staring in the direction whence came an echo of jeering laughter, taunting voices, and trampling feet, — a tumult of noise which was immediately embodied in a mob, who swept down the wide street surrounding an advancing horseman. Through the midst of the shouted abuse which chiefly concerned his rumored opposition to Dare, Cornish rode slowly. Erect and stately, he restrained his irritated horse, showing no sign of seeing or hearing his assailants, and obviously declining to gratify them by an attempt to escape.

Perhaps this apparent invulnerability, perhaps the sight of Dare at the window from which Edith had shrunk away, instigated the roughs to a further display of animosity. Somebody caught up a handful of the refuse which littered the place, and flung it at Cornish. It struck his horse, which, already nervous, shied violently, and threw him to the ground.

Edith sprang to the door, but Dare passed her, with an imperative —

"Stay here!"

The rabble had closed, half delighted, half dismayed, around Cornish's prostrate figure.

Dare thrust them aside.

"Stand back, you curs!" he cried fiercely.

"Curs?" yelled a savage voice. "It be for you we bark, — because he works agin you!"

"Do you think this disgraceful outbreak will help my work? I who labor among you night and day for the law and order which he represents here! Did you expect me to tolerate such an attack on him? I am ashamed that my teaching has so failed with you. Go home! Let me hear no more of this, — or, by the name of my Master, I will leave you to your fate, as He left the chosen people who would not understand his message."

They slunk away, half sullen, half afraid, wholly subdued by the passionate rebuke of the man whose devotion had won him sovereignty among them.

Cornish had risen while Dare was speaking. One of his tormentors apologetically brought him his cap. Another deferentially led up his horse, whose flight had been stopped. Mrs. Brown volubly proffered a glass of wine.

But Cornish heeded none of them. Dust-stained, very pale, visibly shaken by his fall, he confronted Dare with a steadfastness beyond the imitation of the "King of the Town," flushed and triumphant though the latter was, with consciousness of power and generous use of it.

"I have to thank you for your protection," Cornish said clearly, and laid his hand on his horse's bridle.

The still terrified animal recoiled, and Dare interposed eagerly.

"You are not fit to ride yet"— he paused, for Edith came forward from the doorway, and Cornish started sharply.

"My horse will be quiet when I have

mounted," he said. "Miss Lorimer, I regret that you should " —

"My horse is here also," she interrupted. "Please take me home with you!"

"Will you permit me to ride with you also, Miss Lorimer?" Dare entreated. "Some of those fellows are in an ugly mood."

Cornish swung himself into the saddle with an alertness of which the moment before he had seemed incapable.

"Mr. Dare will be a safer escort, Miss Lorimer," he said, and, lifting his cap, he rode down the street.

But Edith's anxiety was too keen to be repulsed by his desertion.

With a hurried good-by to Mrs. Brown, she allowed Dare to assist her in mounting; when he followed her, however, as she turned away, she glanced at him impatiently.

"I wish you would not come," she exclaimed. "You must understand how hard it was for him to thank you just now. Why do you force yourself upon him?"

"Because he may need me. He is hurt; he is scarcely able to keep his seat."

Nor could she dispute this assertion; for as Cornish passed beyond the staring, straggling town his horse's pace slackened, his upright figure slouched wearily, — and three miles of shelterless road lay between him and Ludlow!

Her lips quivered, as her gaze followed him.

"Don't fear," Dare said gently. "He will hold out, I think, — he was always plucky!"

Some subtle tone in his voice for an instant disputed her watching of that drooping rider. The dark eyes which confronted her hasty look were very soft.

"Did n't I tell you that we were chums for years?" he murmured. "Did n't you guess that, though he hates me, my desire to be friends again is not altogether self-interest?"

Vaguely Edith was touched; but, as he spoke, Cornish swayed in the saddle, and his horse stood still.

"He will fall!" she exclaimed, and was rapidly beside him.

Cornish drew himself erect.

"You have overtaken me!" he said, with a stiff, white smile.

"Don't speak! Don't try to hide from us that you are hurt. Let us ride with you," she entreated brokenly.

His glance wandered to the compassionate enemy close at his other hand, ready to catch his bridle should it slip from his relaxing grasp.

"There is not much wrong with me," he muttered, "and you must wish to ride faster."

She did not answer. Nor did either of them speak again during the slow length of those three miles. Mechanically Cornish returned the sentry's salute as they entered the post gateway, and advanced up the parade rigid and straight as a man in a trance.

But he passed Tom Lorimer's door, and that astonished officer's greeting, without sign, while his companions paused.

"Not you!" Edith exclaimed when Dare would have gone on. "Tom! Major Cornish has had a bad fall."

Tom sprang away before her words were fully uttered.

Cornish had halted at his own quarters, and was slowly climbing down from the saddle. But as he stood upright he staggered, fell helplessly into Tom's stalwart embrace, and fainted away.

Dare rushed forward. Dorothy broke into a confusion of questions, and Edith, struggling with her impotent longing to follow them, was bitterly resentful that, when the two men carried Cornish into the house, his unconscious head lay on his enemy's breast.

She trembled violently, and when Dorothy, perceiving this, led her to the drawing-room and forced her gently into an armchair, she burst into tears.

Dorothy's tenderness soon evoked a history of the afternoon, and of her resolve to abandon the singing class, and they were more at ease with each other than they had been for some time. Tom, however, remained absent, and Dorothy presently sent Edith to bed, promising that he should bring her news of Cornish's condition as soon as he returned.

An hour later Tom knocked at his sister's door, and thrust in his kindly countenance.

"A dislocated shoulder and a couple of fractured ribs," he declared cheerfully. "Blount says that every step his horse made must have hurt him confoundedly."

"How is he now?"

"As comfortable as a man who treats broken bones with so little respect can hope to be. But his 'striker' is a dull sort, so I am going back to stay the night with him."

"That is good of you, Tom, dear."

He received her caress affably.

"Dare is the fellow who should be surgeon's assistant," he said. "He cleared out, however, when Cornish began to revive. Admitted frankly that the sight of him would vex the patient. Queer chap!"

He walked to the door.

"Go to sleep, child!" he exclaimed. "You look almost as spent as Cornish does. By the way, he sent you a message. His apologies for making a scene!"

Owing to the desire of Cornish, the assault to which his accident was due was not officially noted, and such rumors of the facts as reached Ludlow were merely whispered at the barracks. The surgeon's verdict on the commanding officer's case was a fortnight's confinement to his quarters. But he proved an invalid upon whom his exasperated medical adviser found it impossible to execute sentence. Within a week of his accident, he appeared at his office, carrying an arm in a sling, yet manifesting, Tom reported, his habitual disposition to overwork himself and every one else.

Late that afternoon Edith, who was reading on the veranda, glanced up at the sound of a slow step, and saw him approaching.

"I have a vague idea that you meant to

be very kind to me the other day, and that I was churlish," he said, smiling, as he took the chair which she drew forward, with a murmured greeting. "Will you forgive me?"

Would she forgive him? She who was so glad to see him, even thus white and worn, that she knew a gladness out of all proportion to what was expected of her must be shining in her happy eyes. She turned them away from him.

"It is hard to forgive myself for having been powerless to help you," she answered softly. "I shall always dislike those special three miles!"

"You will soon have more agreeable associations with a ride you take so often."

"I dare say I shall not go that way again this summer," she exclaimed, coloring. "Tom and Mrs. Blount have rendered it impossible for me to continue my singing class at Silverton."

"You have given it up?"

"I could not ride over without either of them, and they deserted."

"Then it was not to the wishes of your friends that you yielded?" Cornish said sharply. "How does Mr. Dare endure the failure of one of his projects?"

"I have not seen him since the afternoon when he " —

"When he magnanimously extended the ægis of his protection to me " —

Cornish paused. The nervous irritation of his manner steadied into sternness, as he rose, confronting somebody behind Edith.

She guessed, as she turned, that the new-comer was Dare. He stood in the long drawing-room window, gravely graceful as a cavalier by Velasquez — if it could be imagined that Velasquez might have painted a cavalier in cow-boy flannels and buckskins, instead of knightly velvet and steel.

"The 'striker' told me that I should find your brother with you, Miss Lorimer," he said. "But Major Cornish will be yet more satisfactory, if I may speak to him for a moment on business."

Edith assented, smiling perfunctorily.

"I am at my office every morning until noon," Cornish began coldly.

But Dare interrupted him with an impetuous sweetness of look and tone which touched Edith despite her annoyance at his coming.

"You do not seem fit for office work yet, and I should not ask it of you. My business is merely to request a favor for Sergeant Robin of Troop E."

"Who was tried by court martial yesterday for overstaying a furlough, and losing money at poker which belonged to his comrades?"

"He swears that he was drugged and robbed."

"The usual defense."

"I know it to be true in this case."

"Testimony should have been submitted before the conclusion of the court martial."

"I was only sure of it an hour ago."

"The officers who tried him will undoubtedly receive it."

"This is my difficulty," Dare exclaimed. "The man who drugged and robbed him possesses enormous influence among the worst set in Silverton. I hope to so overwhelm him with evidence of guilt that he may be forced to leave the town, but I am as yet unprepared. As you know, there is no civil authority there, and I must work *sub rosa*. Will you not take my word that Robin's sentence is undeserved?"

"No!"

The single syllable sounded short and distinct as a pistol shot, and Dare recoiled as though he had received it. The two men faced each other dumbly.

"You will permit this trooper to suffer unjustly that you may insult me?" Dare demanded.

"It would be irregular in any case to remit sentence for reasons which cannot be made public."

"Will you hear my statement of them?"

"My decision would be unchanged."

Dare struck his hands together passionately.

"Miss Lorimer!" he began.

But Cornish interposed haughtily.

"No intercession will affect me."

"It is hard to see one's own punishment fall upon other shoulders," Dare muttered, and walked toward the house.

Cornish leaned his unhurt arm on the chair from which he had risen when Dare arrived.

"Wait," he said, his color fading with every husky word. "If you will have your evidence ready to produce within a week, I will withhold sentence until then."

Dare turned. He made a step nearer, but Cornish neither moved nor lifted his bent gaze.

"Thank you," Dare said gently, and was gone.

Cornish sank into the chair.

"I seem destined to make a fool of myself in your presence," he faltered impatiently.

"When a man conquers his own heart, he is not called a fool," Edith answered with a tremulous smile which was very sweet.

"He is called greater than he who taketh a city."

His look dwelt on her, and his tired eyes filled with light.

"That is the first approval I have ever won from you," he murmured.

"Would you like to win more?" she asked, flushing daintily over all her drooping face. "I hear my brother coming, and he will beg you to stay for dinner; go home instead, — you are a very ghost."

"And only sorrowful ghosts walk abroad, — do they not?" he said, lifting a ribbon which hung from her belt and putting it softly down again. "I shall take this happy ghost to quarters."

He rose as Tom emerged from the drawing-room window, and went to meet him.

IV

THAT evening after dinner Edith obtained the details of Sergeant Robin's case from her brother, who had been presiding officer at the court martial.

The sergeant was a veteran of six years' service, possessing a creditable record in a couple of Indian campaigns. Cards and drink had been familiar stumbling blocks during the earlier portion of his career, but his superiors supposed them overcome when a sergeant's chevrons were bestowed upon him just before his troop was ordered to Ludlow. At Silverton he had, however, fallen under evil influences. His captain was patient with him until an overstayed furlough, and the loss of money entrusted to him by comrades, constituted faults that could not be condoned. He had admitted the facts of both charges to the court martial board and had proved unable to produce testimony for his defense that he had been drugged and robbed. Therefore a severe sentence was submitted to Cornish for approval. The man Dawson, in whose dance-hall and lodging-house Robin had lost the money, was a power for evil at the settlement, and an obstinate foe to Dare's reforms. Tom, though glad that the sergeant's accusation should have another chance of corroboration, was inclined to believe Dare's certainty of its truth inspired by a personal desire to expose Dawson, and the secrecy requested while he pursued his investigations savored of the *coup de théâtre*, always somewhat characteristic of Dare's methods. Furthermore, Tom, with a mischievous smile, attributed Cornish's postponement of the sentence entirely to feminine wishes.

When Edith warmly defended Cornish's sense of justice, he dropped the subject with prompt awkwardness, in obedience to a signal from his wife.

Edith also beheld the signal, and without resentment.

Then she went to her piano, and dreamed away the remainder of the evening, singing with a sweet conviction that through two open windows those tender old ballads were listened to by Cornish in solitude, after a different fashion from that of Tom and Dorothy, who blithely teased each other across a chess-board.

A week elapsed, — a week during which Cornish grew daily stronger, and the surgeon, attributing complacently this improvement to his closer observance of medical restrictions, prophesied his speedily complete recovery. They were days in which he displayed an ingenuity as to the frequency and naturalness of his meetings with Edith, which amused Mrs. Blount and Dorothy, being so evidently of love, not of necessity; for at a three-company post all lives are lived in enforced propinquity.

The morning came at last, ending the week which Cornish had granted to Dare for the production of his evidence in favor of Sergeant Robin, and Edith, walking up the parade, was reminded of it by seeing Dare issue from headquarters.

He was so absorbed in his thoughts that he did not perceive her until she paused.

"Good-morning," she exclaimed, smiling. "I hope your presence here thus early means good news for poor Robin?"

"The best," he answered briskly. "Your brother has agreed to call together the court martial board that I may read to them the confession I extracted from Dawson. It clears the sergeant of everything except folly, — an attribute so widespread that if soldiers were dismissed for its manifestation," he added gayly, "our standing army would soon cease to exist!"

"I hope that Dawson is definitely vanquished?"

"At all events he is gone, and his departure was hastened by the urgency of his neighbors. I fear, indeed, that his influence has not all departed with him. But," he interrupted himself, smiling, "it is thankless to conjure misgivings after such a victory! May I come in for an instant?"

Edith assented. He was so instinct with energy and achievement, and both were so nobly unselfish, that her sympathy inclined to him even more than its wont. Yet she shrank, while she blamed her shrinking, from the chance of another encounter between him and Cornish. Did she not know that only by similar encounters could they reach that mutual comprehension she desired for them? It was mere cowardice to dread the momentary eclipse of that new brightness in two grave blue eyes.

Her attention wandered from what Dare was saying, as she preceded him to the drawing-room, and was recalled when she confronted his glance half sad, half amused. Did he guess her unwillingness?

He was speaking of her quondam class, which had appeared successfully at his recent preachings.

"We sing only the most generally known

hymns, and we hope when the whole audience become familiar with the airs, that they will join the refrains. Unless you have heard such a chorus you can have no conception how glorious it is — three or four hundred voices singing their Creator's praise under his everlasting stars!"

Dare's smile was radiant, but something chilled her, listening, — perhaps the abiding thought of a nature in whose depths and heights was silence.

"Isn't such a display of fervor more emotional than real?" she asked with involuntary coldness.

Dare's brilliant look grew troubled.

"We must win them through their emotions!" he exclaimed. "What power do you imagine conscientious conviction has over the lives of that wild flock of mine? Their emotions rule them, and I can but seek to turn those emotions from the paths of sin to the service of God!"

He had risen. He was pale. His voice vibrated.

Edith was aghast before the feeling she had aroused.

"I beg your pardon very humbly," she entreated. "You must know how far I am from daring to criticise a mission I so honor as I do yours. I meant only to ask you whether you thought that emotion likely to produce enduring results?"

"When I am most hopeful," Dare said dreamily, — his mood had changed again; he leaned on the mantelshelf; his vague gaze touched her without perceiving her, — "I believe that my efforts may be the sunshine and the rain, to which God gives the power to bring forth his harvest. Yet why should I hope that work of mine" —

"Forgive me!" she murmured. "It is not your work or your aim that I doubt!"

"But I doubt them!" he said very low. "Is it God's glory for which I serve or for my own? Is it not pride and triumph to me, after the shipwreck I have made, to know that I can sway this townful of humanity as I wish? Though the road by which

I lead them is God's road, do I not exult in their leadership for my honor?"

"No, no, no!" Edith cried with soft vehemence. "Such doubts are fatigue, overwork or — or" — she faltered, and the tears were on her lashes, — "or the pain of ' a wound from the hand of a friend '!"

Dare recovered himself with a swiftness she had seen him achieve once before.

"It is a very kind hand," he said, smiling, "so kind that even the wounds it inflicts are clean and pure as a surgeon's, which are for healing, not for hurting!" He hesitated; "I wish" — he resumed again as he picked up his broad felt hat — "I failed to see Major Cornish to-day, but your brother tells me that he is recovering."

"He talks of riding this afternoon, though Dr. Blount objects."

"He was generous to me about Robin's case," Dare said slowly. "Yet he has no faith in me; and when we were boys — ah! and years afterward, my word was law to him! You, who are more than worthy of all trust, — you cannot conceive the pain of meeting his honest eyes, and knowing that you can never bring back their lost faith!"

"But you will! He is so true that he must recognize truth when he sees it clearly."

"Does not his truth perceive my falsehood? And if I never see pardon in eyes which are so like Rosamond's — shall I ever see forgiveness in hers?"

He was gone swiftly, leaving Edith an aching legacy of compassion for the blackest anguish a soul may suffer; one which she knew that some of the stoutest souls who ever fought for the world's salvation have found their deadliest foe — which is indeed the shadow haunting all enthusiasts, the great darkness of self doubt.

Late in the afternoon Mrs. Blount and Dorothy returned from an expedition to Silverton. Edith was making tea for them when Tom entered, and delivered himself at once of the result of the court martial.

The confession, which Dare had exacted from Dawson, fully corroborated Robin's story, and he had been sent back to his duty with a rebuke and a warning.

Those were the facts of the proceedings, but Tom's eloquence was not limited to facts. He was again possessed by that confident admiration for Dare which had been banished by Cornish's story and his own consequent fears as to the results of his sister's zeal. This relapse had been imminent since Edith's abandonment of the singing class, and the energy, acumen, and courage Dare had now displayed brought it to a climax. Not only was the proof of Dawson's guilt so complete that public opinion had banished him with a haste which left his affairs to be settled by underlings, but certain leading citizens, who had come over to the court martial, had added to Dare's brief statement details which they declared made him yet more absolutely " king of the town." Among those rough frontiersmen, personal fearlessness was the ideal common to those who were able to appreciate the high purpose of regeneration which had inspired his single-handed defiance of a notorious ruffian, and to those who could only admire the dauntlessness which accomplished its object careless of danger.

"An object that embraces wider interests than Robin's acquittal, which was merely the point of a wedge to split up an influence destructive to the community," Tom continued gravely. "The expulsion of such a rascal as Dawson is a long stride toward the establishment of law and civil authority, for which Dare is urging a petition to the legislature at Helena."

"Will not that end his dictatorship?" Edith asked, remembering, with a flutter at her throat, his morbid self-torment of the morning.

"That is a consideration beneath his reckoning. But the better class at Silverton are anxious for his safety. They fear that he is exposed to a vengeance, likely to have been entrusted by Dawson to members of his gang, as evil of instinct and as sure of shot as himself."

"Cannot they protect Dare?" Edith exclaimed, indignantly. "Anxiety is n't very real which finds no expression beyond words."

"How can you protect a man with such a mission and such a temperament?" Tom cried fervently. "He answers their warnings as Martin Luther used — 'If I die I die; and there is one preacher less in the world; but while I live I will serve God as He directs me.'"

They were gathered about the tea table, their hearts stirred by the story of this war against evil, and by the words of the great reformer, which echo down the centuries with his triumph.

Even Edith was jarred, as by a discordant note, when Cornish's voice said formally from the doorway —

"May I come in?"

"Ah, Major, glad to see you! Of course Jackson has told you that Robin is acquitted?" Tom exclaimed, too eager to abandon his subject. "I wish you had heard the story of Dawson's defeat from those who saw it."

"Were you not at the court martial, Major Cornish?" Mrs. Blount asked.

"The court martial took place while I was ill," Cornish answered. "This meeting was simply to annul their former sentence, and my presence was unnecessary;" he hesitated, and added harshly, "I trust the sergeant received the severe reprimand he deserved?"

Tom assured him that Robin had seemed properly impressed by the narrowness of his escape. Then they talked on indifferent topics, with a sense that their attempted lightness was heavily weighted. Mrs. Blount speedily departed. Tom and Dorothy strolled to the doorstep with her, and Cornish looked at Edith beseechingly.

"Will you come out on the veranda? I

— I have not been able to see you alone to-day."

Presently they leaned against the railings side by side, and stared away across scraggy intervening "buttes" to the far-stretching prairie — that prairie desolate as the ocean, and inspiring with the same conviction of eternity and infiniteness the vague longings of humanity.

"You think that I am unjust?" he said.

"Yes — and I am very sorry."

"For him?"

"For both of you. I hoped, the other evening, that you had begun to feel the nobleness of his motives."

"I believed that he would accomplish the task he undertook, and justice to Robins compelled me to give him time," Cornish said hurriedly. "I half knew that I got your approval on false pretenses, but — " he left his sentence unfinished, and stood erect. "I shall never trust him," he ended sternly.

"It adds a bitterness to his sorrow that he cannot recall the belief you once gave him."

"Can he recall those whom my belief thrust into the way of his cruelty?"

He looked down at her fair upturned face, and his eyes adored her.

"He has taken so much from me!" he muttered. "I am mad with fear that he will take you too!"

"Me? — Me!"

Such a passion of protestation and denial was in those short syllables that Cornish grew white with a rapture whose sudden sweetness dizzied him.

He caught her hands to his breast.

"I love you! I — I love you!" he stammered. "And you — ?"

"Ah, you know!" she murmured, a soft thrill of laughter between two sobs. "I told you first!"

When they imparted their news to Tom and Dorothy it was declared to be no news at all! What the garrison society said of it varied in form according to individual character, but the import of placid satisfaction was universal. Most of them, indeed, had been sure of the engagement and of their approval of it, before Edith and Cornish had approached such certainty.

"All the world loves a lover," and the small world at Ludlow was amiably disposed to give these two every opportunity for spending the largest possible proportion of the glorious summer hours together. Among many plans, a riding party was proposed to a waterfall in a gulch among the foothills a couple of miles beyond Silverton. There was question as to the distance being within Cornish's present strength, but he, having essayed a shorter ride, was confident of his endurance.

Half a dozen of them set forth accordingly — a judicious number, Mrs. Blount agreed with Dorothy, who was not going; a number from which the lovers might wander off at pleasure, without feeling that they thus forced as absolute and less enchanting a *solitude à deux* upon their companions.

No Italian sky could have been more radiant than the cloudless blue above them. The breeze, which floated with soft sighs from nowhere in particular, was instinct of that wondrous Montana vitality which is like the stir of renewed youth to sluggish pulses; while to pulses bounding with a thrill yet keener than its own, it added another sweetness to one of life's most exquisite hours.

The waterfall formed part of a swift little river, which was shut in between high banks overgrown by such wild greenery that the riding party were compelled to tether their horses at the entrance of the gulch and follow its course on foot to their destination. But Edith doubted whether Cornish was equal to so rough a scramble as this meant, and she found no difficulty in persuading him that half an hour alone together was worth a greater loss than the view they sacrificed!

They allowed the others to wander on unregretted. She sat beside him, while he lay on the grass with her hand in his clasp, and the unutterable content of his pale face flooded her soul with the most exultant sense of power that a good woman can know — for such women are all individualists! However keen their intellect, however virile their energy, no widely diffused influence of talent and character is more than a cold substitute for the sovereignty of one heart chosen to reign over!

Throughout the life which stretched before them there would be moods of his strong silent nature which she must divine for his happiness. But she felt confident of her magic as his fingers quivered, when she laid her other hand softly over them.

"I am a dull fellow," he murmured, looking up at her with eyes that spoke love after a fashion whose eloquence has found no equal language in words, since the world and love-making began together. "I am dull and dumb — with rough places that may hurt you sometimes — yet — yet — "

"Mine own," she answered softly. "And

I have a wonderful esteem for my own property!"

She bent a little nearer to him, smiling.

"Isn't it absurd, or what the old novels would call 'unmaidenly,' to confess that I have felt that you belonged to me — almost from the first? — Now you know why I have lectured you and hectored you! All you did — what you said — what you did n't say, it was all mine, of which I was proud — or otherwise, — but my very own!"

Cornish had risen to his knees. He sought to draw to his the lips which made such confession. But she started away from him.

"There is somebody," she exclaimed. Then added in a changed tone, "Look — he is that man Dawson."

Cornish turned sharply, and saw a figure slinking through the underbrush on the opposite side of the stream.

Edith shivered.

"Why is he here? They say he vowed vengeance against Mr. Dare — and it is almost a week since he was expelled from the town."

"His object is probably to keep up communication with those who are settling his business matters. Vengeance which talks loud does n't often come to action," Cornish said, smiling.

The serpent must have been unavoidably combative who could disturb his Paradise just then!

"Mr. Dare should be warned," she began nervously.

But he would not permit the thought of Dare to haunt her.

He lifted her hand, and kissed each white finger.

"I knew that I was yours, to make happy, or to make miserable, from the moment your blessed touch brought me to my senses the night of the sermon," he murmured.

And straightway there descended upon them that sweet oblivion, to which most of the world owes too dear a debt for blame or carping.

Their companions returned, gayly scornful, and extolling the beauties of the waterfall.

They strolled leisurely back to the horses. But so soon as they had emerged from the gulch they perceived that something nearer and darker than the coming night was rushing across the western sky. A storm was close upon them, and everybody was suddenly in a hurry.

Yet the haste of the tempest was swifter than theirs, and it overtook them when they had only reached the outskirts of Silverton. A chaos of wind and water and electricity enveloped them. The frightened horses halted, bending their heads, and passively opposing their riders' efforts to urge them further.

"We must lead them," Cornish exclaimed. "Thank God, shelter is near!"

He dismounted and, taking Edith's bridle with his own in his unhurt hand, he dragged the two horses after him toward a house which loomed dimly before them.

The other men followed his example for the brief distance that intervened.

So bewildering was the tumult, and so altered the aspect of familiar things by the weirdly changed atmosphere, that they had become confused as to their bearings. The women, clinging to the saddles, were barely able to keep their seats, while the men stumbled and slipped with the difficulty of their footing, and the inert resistance of the animals they led.

A door was flung open in the building they were struggling to reach. Against the background of lighted interior stood a tall silhouette. It was Dare.

He welcomed them gladly, sending a couple of boys to bestow the horses under a shed, declaring that the storm was too violent to endure and in the mean time he was very happy that they must accept what poor hospitality he could offer.

Talking gayly, with the sense of escape from the flashing danger outside, they entered the big club-room behind the store, where three or four loungers sprang to their feet in decorous shyness before the presence of ladies.

As the door shut behind them, Cornish, who had walked away to the further end of the veranda, flung himself on a bench.

But Edith, lingering unseen, followed him swiftly, and sank down beside him.

"Go in!" he exclaimed, starting. "You cannot wish to stay here."

"You are to know, now and always, that where you are there I shall wish to be," she whispered.

He drew her close to him with passionate remorse.

"Forgive me!" he muttered. "Sweet! sweet!"

Then he rose, lifting her also.

"We will go in together," he said.

"Not if it hurts you! I am so wet already that I shall be no worse for getting wetter. And I believe the rain has ceased!"

She was right. The rain was gone as suddenly as it had come. The wind, however, still blew her loosened hair about the fair, smiling face which the lightning showed him.

"We are very well out here," she began gallantly. But the words died on her lips as there pierced sharply through the roar of the wind and the crash of the thunder that cry most dreaded of all earth's clamors of distress: —

"Fire! Fire! Fire!"

Except on a ship at sea that sound is never so terrible as in a prairie town, built of such flimsy materials as adds each another fuel to the racing blaze which reaches it.

At the first shriek the house door was thrown open, and several men, bounding across the porch, vanished into the lurid darkness. An instant afterward Dare, Tom Lorimer, and Gwynne appeared.

"The rain has stopped!" Dare cried with dismay.

"The town must be well drenched, however," Tom exclaimed. "The water pelted down on us as from a cloud-burst."

"It cannot have done more than wet the

surface of those buildings, which are scorched to tinder with the drought," Dare said absently, and listening the while to the outcries whose volume seemed to increase as the storm rapidly lessened.

"I must leave you. You will be able to return to the post soon now—"

"The ladies will be safe here, and we cannot desert our neighbors while they may need our help." Tom hesitated, glancing at the two figures motionless among the shadows.

"Right, Lorimer!" Cornish exclaimed, advancing. "We must know the extent of danger to the town;" he looked directly to Dare. "We have hose and a small hand engine that can be got here within half an hour."

"Thank you. I will let you know immediately," Dare answered, springing down the steps.

"Wait," Cornish said with effort. "Miss Lorimer desires that you should be told that Dawson is near — probably in town."

Dare paused, and glanced back, while the light from the doorway shone on his resolute, handsome face.

"The town is full of my friends," he said. "I am armed, and " — a gleam which was not saintly flashed in his eyes, — "I am as sure a shot as he is!"

He rushed off, followed by Gwynne, who was as wild at the propinquity of a fire as most grown-up boys of more years than he had attained.

The others remained, watching the gathering of a crowd now revealed by flames which burst forth from a large drinking-saloon that had been struck by lightning.

Dare's store stood some distance beyond its nearest neighbor toward the hills, at that end of the street furthest from the little river between which and the fire a triple line of water carriers was forming.

Presently, neither Tom nor Cornish could resist the contagion of excitement, and they, too, vanished among those shadowy, swaying figures. A moment later flames darted from the houses on either side of that in which the fire had begun, while the roof of one just opposite blazed fiercely under the burning wreckage flung upon it by the wind.

Almost simultaneously young Gwynne appeared, bounding toward the shed where the horses were sheltered.

"The Major has sent me for the engine and a dozen fellows of Troop E," he cried, and swept by them again on horseback, waving his cap.

Mrs. Blount and Edith were alone, with the big open rooms empty behind them, for everything masculine was waging the fight, whose loss or whose winning meant life or death to the settlement. Half an hour, during which nobody came to them, elapsed, while they strained sight and hearing to measure the increasing danger.

Then they were aware of the steady gallop of Gwynne's reinforcements, the shouts of welcome which received them, and the hurried separation of the crowd for the stretching of the hose.

They had just rejoiced at the rush of water upon the flames, which betokened the working of the engine, when they saw a couple of men advancing toward them, supporting another.

"Who are you?" Mrs. Blount cried, while Edith's voice seemed suddenly as still as her heart.

"Bob Frost has broke his arm," somebody answered. "The doctor chap from Ludlow said to bring him here, and he would set it after a bit."

"I'm the 'doctor chap's' wife, which is next best to being himself," Mrs. Blount declared gayly. "I know enough to make this poor fellow more comfortable."

With which she supervised the installation of her dazed and grimy patient in a large chair, and began to cut up his shirt sleeve.

Edith, in the mean time, inspired by her energy, found the way to the kitchen, and rebuilt the fire there, with a view to providing hot water for probable necessities.

Bob Frost's comrades promptly left him to these willing ministrants, and his wits cleared under the stimulant of some whiskey which Mrs. Blount fetched from the bar.

He proved able presently to soothe their terror at a tremendous explosion that rattled every window in the house.

"Never fear, ladies," he exclaimed cheerfully; "it's just dynamite, which Dare got from the mines to blow up a shanty or two, and so starve out the fire."

He proceeded to "prophesy smooth things" as to the diminution of the danger from these measures, the abatement of the wind, and the good help of the engine.

"Them soldiers works fine," he continued, when his eloquence was limbered by the interest of his audience, and the strength of his potation. "Dare, he sings out, after he had watched them a bit, 'There, boys,' he says, 'look at them chaps; we have got the will to work like them, but they have got the way too! That is what law and order does for men, — it teaches the way to them that has the will, and that is what we are going to learn when we get into tackle with the "big wigs" of the state government.' Dare is a great fellow for 'law and order,'" Bob added reflectively; "but he is making us all so mild and moral on his own hook, that when he gets the sheriff and the mayor he wants for us, they will find he ain't left them anything to do!"

A consummation scarcely yet reached, however near Bob's optimistic admiration of his leader believed it.

As he spoke, the comparative stillness which had followed the explosion was smitten through by pistol shots, and then by such an outbreak of yells as though all the devils of rage and fury had burst into utterance.

"Some sneak thief has paid a high price for trying to steal from the goods piled up in the street," Bob asserted confidently. "Dare will quiet things, but even he could n't save such a skunk at such a time, I guess."

Edith returned to the porch, shivering with a dread which this explanation did not allay, and which made her watching almost unendurable.

Between her and the fire, which had ceased to gain ground, lay the scene of this disturbance, she thought, for she saw a hurrying to and fro which apparently had no concern with the yet urgent battle against the flames. After a moment, half a dozen figures detached themselves from this group, and moved toward her, carrying a prostrate body.

It was for her one of those spaces in which a soul neither prays nor reasons in its anguish of suspense.

She recognized her brother hastening forward.

"My poor girl," he began.

"Quickly!" she gasped.

"Cornish is safe," Tom exclaimed. "But Dare — We have had a horrible scene, and I cannot spare you and Mrs. Blount the end of it."

"What has happened?" Edith tried to ask, while each heart-beat was a thanksgiving which for an instant could understand no new pain.

"Dawson was there. He disputed Dare's order to blow up his place. Dare told him to clear out or he would have him locked up, and the scoundrel shot him."

"Shot Dare!"

"And after a time, when it seemed likely that he would be torn in pieces by those maddened fellows, he shot himself."

"But Dare?"

"Blount says he is dying. They are bringing him here."

Tom entered the house, while Edith sank on a bench and watched that slowly advancing group evolve from shadows to substance as they came within the light of the open doors and windows behind her.

Faint with horror and compassion, she sat, motionless, as Dare's inanimate figure was borne carefully up the steps and into the house. Dr. Blount and several others followed closely. Then she watched no further, for Cornish stumbled forward.

She caught his cold hand as he was passing her, unseeing. He submitted to the soft insistence which drew him down on the bench beside her. But, except that his fingers clung to hers, he showed no heed of her, and, leaning on the window ledge behind the bench, he gazed into the lighted bedroom where Dare had been laid.

Presently, facing this point of view, gathered others excluded by Tom's repetition of Dr. Blount's command that nobody further should be admitted to disturb his patient.

Dare lay propped up with pillows, and had regained consciousness. Edith saw him smile gratefully as Mrs. Blount came deftly to her husband's assistance, and, after a moment, through the heavy silence which had fallen upon every one, she heard his low tones quite audibly.

"Give me up, Doctor! We both know that you are wasting time, and I can spare none of what is left me."

With a murmur of acquiescence the surgeon gently drew the coverlid over the torn shirt and blood-stained bandages.

Dare looked up at the men who stood around him, — the men who represented the best element in Silverton, and in whose countenances was written sore dismay.

"Be of good cheer, little flock. Neither be ye afraid," he said, and his voice rang clear as in his preaching. "I think you know whose words those were, and at what parting they were spoken? — when the Lord Jesus Christ left his work for them to continue who felt so unequal to it. They are his words now, not mine! It is his work now, which is left in your hands, not mine! His work, which He has taken from me because He sees that I am unworthy to carry it further."

A great sob broke from the burly manager of the "Yankee Doodle."

"Don't you say that, Dare! Don't you try to make us believe the Lord sees no clearer! He wants you for Himself — and that's a fact!"

A light, half awe, half triumph, glorified Dare's white face.

"His mercy is infinite," he murmured. "Yet you must believe, as I do, that He is taking me from temptation. I have labored for you, and prayed for you; I have brought you thus far out of the bondage of lawlessness. But a day is near when my power among you would diminish, — when I should be merely a citizen under the law, — no more the King of the Town," he smiled. "And the Lord knows that I should not like to abdicate. Hush!" he added imperatively. "We have some work still to do together, and it must be done quickly. Am I talking too much?" — he interrupted himself at a warning from Dr. Blount. "My time for silence is very near."

The radiant serenity of his glance seemed to confront Cornish, though he was unaware of that tense watching. With an inarticulate exclamation Cornish rose, and, yet clasping Edith's hand, forced their way through the group behind them to the end of the veranda.

"Not one falter! not one regret, except for them," he murmured, pausing. "That cannot be hypocrisy? Say something to me to bend my stubbornness, — to crush my doubts."

She clung to him dumbly. He was ghastly with fatigue, with the pain of his half healed hurt, — yet more worn with the struggle of his stern uprightness, which must be justly convinced before it would yield to the yearning of old affection. But what need for her to speak, when through his soul echoed another voice?

"From the moment we reached the fire until he was shot," Cornish went on brokenly, "every word, every order proved him a leader of men. We were tools for his use, — all of us. Now, face to face with death, which surely makes souls honest, he is — this! Yet he is the man I have such reason to hate, — whose life for years was a record of shame and worthlessness."

He leaned his head against the wall behind him, and shut his eyes.

"God help me," he muttered. "Nothing but bitter repentance could make a change as wide as between hell and heaven, — yet I cannot forget —"

She put her arm over his shoulder. The tears were racing down her cheeks.

"My poor love," he said, "you always believed in him — tell me what to do?"

"You know, dearest — dearest — you know!"

He kissed her.

"Come!" he exclaimed.

Again they paused beside the window, where the watchers made place for them.

Dare was signing some papers, with a faintly amused wonder at the shaken characters.

"There is a certain pathos in that signature," he said. "It may compel the attention of the legislators at Helena, — and, oh! my friends, whom I am leaving, — never forget that the closer you live to law and order, the more real will be your liberty!"

His voice failed. He listened wistfully to the sob-broken assurances that, for his sake, the roughest of them would be as lambs in the fold of civil authority to which he consigned them.

His glance wandered from the little circle, about the wide, bare room.

"Is there any one you want to see?" Dr. Blount asked.

"Somebody who will not come," Dare murmured wearily.

Cornish shivered. He opened the door and walked swiftly to Dare's side.

The dying eyes were lifted to the living eyes that were scarcely less haggard, — perhaps, for that instant, those two wide-set souls so strongly knit together beheld each other as they shall hereafter in truth and verity.

Cornish sank to his knees, and his hand closed over Dare's limp fingers.

"Rosamond — " Dare's lips still moved, but the words were inaudible. His lids drooped heavily.

Dr. Blount leaned forward and touched Cornish's shoulder.

But Dare's eyes opened again.

"I believe in the forgiveness of sins," he said, and smiled — that mysterious sweet smile, which if it be not the dawn of Heaven, then is our faith vain.

www.ingramcontent.com/pod-product-compliance
Lightning Source LLC
Chambersburg PA
CBHW030319170426
43202CB00009B/1066